THE CORONATION OF KING CHARLES

The Triumph of Universal Harmony

A Masque

JOHN HUNT PUBLISHING

First published by O-Books, 2021
O-Books is an imprint of John Hunt Publishing Ltd., 3 East St., Alresford,
Hampshire SO24 9EE, UK
office@jhpbooks.com
www.johnhuntpublishing.com
www.o-books.com

For distributor details and how to order please visit the 'Ordering' section on our website.

Text copyright: Nicholas Hagger 2020

ISBN: 978 1 78904 476 8
978 1 78904 477 5 (ebook)
Library of Congress Control Number: 2020936356

A CIP catalogue record for this book is available from the British Library.

Design: Stuart Davies

UK: Printed and bound by CPI Group (UK) Ltd, Croydon, CR0 4YY
Printed in North America by CPI GPS partners

We operate a distinctive and ethical publishing philosophy in all areas
of our business, from our global network of authors to production and
worldwide distribution.

THE CORONATION
OF KING CHARLES

The Triumph of Universal Harmony

A Masque

Nicholas Hagger

BOOKS

Winchester, UK
Washington, USA

Also by Nicholas Hagger

Peace for our Time
World State
World Constitution
King Charles the Wise
Visions of England
Fools' Paradise
Selected Letters
Collected Prefaces

"'Masque', a form of amateur histrionic entertainment, originally consisting of dancing and acting in dumb show, the performers being masked, afterwards including dialogue and song, 1562; a dramatic composition for this kind of entertainment, 1605."

The Shorter Oxford English Dictionary

"'Masque', a dramatic and musical entertainment, especially of the 16th and 17th centuries, originally of pantomime, later with metrical dialogue; a dramatic composition for this."

The Concise Oxford Dictionary

"'Pageant', a spectacle arranged for effect; especially a procession or parade with elaborate spectacular display, 1805. Since 1907 applied to celebrations of local history consisting of a series of representations of events and personages connected with the particular place."

The Shorter Oxford English Dictionary

"'Pageant', a brilliant spectacle, especially an elaborate parade; a spectacular procession, or play performed in the open, illustrating historical events."

The Concise Oxford Dictionary

The front cover shows the inside of the Banqueting House, Whitehall, London, built for James I as a venue for masques, with God of the One, whose Divine Light conferred the divine right of kings of David's line (top left), and the ceremonial regalia of King Charles's coronation (bottom right).

I am indebted to Thomas Woodcock, Garter Principal King of Arms of the College of Arms, for checking the Royal Family's descent on pp.57–59 and 67–72.

CONTENTS

Dramatis Personae

Characters in order of appearance:
(* = listed more than once; † = live chorus that could be shown on screen
to reduce the cast)

A. Live cast
King Charles
Prolocutor (Minerva)
Kings and queens (non-speakers)
Chorus of the pageant:
> The entire cast except for King Charles, the Prolocutor and God of the
> One take part in the singing, including:
> Kings and queens
> Archbishop
> Speaker
> Judge
> Doctor
> Military leader
> Butcher
> Journalist
> TV presenter
> Labourer
> Old lady
> Government minister
> Worker
> Soldier
> Road sweeper
> Homeless Londoner
> War victim
> Solomon
> Ben Jonson
> Charles I
> James I
> Shakespeare
> Members of the live choruses listed † below, some of which could be
> shown on screen to reduce the cast
God of the One
Archbishop
Solomon
Ben Jonson
Charles I (non-speaker)

*James I
*Shakespeare
Homeless Londoner
War victim
†Chorus of angry Brexiteers
†Chorus of indignant historical figures
    *Henry VIII
    Shakespeare
    Drake
    Sir Walter Raleigh
    James I
    Nelson
    Wellington
    Earl Haig
    Churchill
†Chorus of the British poor
    Homeless man
    Nurse
    Healthcare worker
    Teaching assistant
    Police officer
    Retired soldier
    Pensioner
†Chorus of the wretched of the Commonwealth
    South African
    Kenyan
    Pakistani
    Canadian
    Jamaican
    Cypriot
    New Zealander
†Chorus of suffering humankind
    American
    European
    African
    Middle Eastern
    Indian
    Australian
    Russian
    Chinese
All choruses not on screen can be drawn from the Chorus of the pageant.

B. On screen (not present in the Banqueting House)
Chorus of UN delegates
  North American
  South American
  European
  Indian
  African
  Australian
  Russian
  Chinese
Chorus of Representatives and Senators of the democratic World State
Chorus of 9 shades of Kings and leaders
  Alfred
  Harold II
  William I, Conqueror
  Henry II
  Henry VIII
  George III
  Lord Palmerston
  Winston Churchill
  Keir Hardie
Chorus of historical leaders from the British Empire and Commonwealth
Chorus of British people
Chorus of the world's united peoples
Chorus of once-suffering peoples
Chorus of 8 distinguished supporters
  Truman
  Eisenhower
  Einstein
  Churchill
  Russell
  Gandhi
  J.F. Kennedy
  Gorbachev

Location:
The Banqueting House, Whitehall, London

*

Music in order of performance:
'David the son of Jesse said' (Hagger), Coronation anthem

'Zadok the Priest'
    Set by Tomkins
    Set by Lawes
    Set by Handel
'I was glad'
    Set by Pigott
'The Lord is a sun and a shield' (Croft)
'Let thy hand be strengthened' (Handel)
'The King shall rejoice' (Handel)
'My heart is inditing' (Handel)
'O Lord, grant the King a long life' (Attwood)
'This is the day that the Lord hath made' (Knyvett)
'Kings shall see and arise' (Bridge)
'O hearken thou' (Elgar)
'*Confortare* (Be strong and play the man)' (Davies)
'Festival *Te Deum*' (Vaughan Williams)
'O taste and see' (Vaughan Williams)
'Behold O God our defender' (Howell)
'Coronation *Te Deum*' (Walton)
'O Lord our Governour' (Willan)

Preface
A Coronation Masque, the Carolingian Age and Universal Harmony

Masques

The early European masques were court entertainments and often celebrated royal marriages. The English masques of the 16th and early 17th centuries were performed in the Banqueting Hall of the Whitehall Palace, often over Christmas or on Twelfth Night, and later in the Banqueting House, which was built between 1619 and 1622 and replaced the Banqueting Hall.

Between 1605 and 1631 Ben Jonson wrote 28 masques (starting with *The Masque of Blackness* and finishing with *Chloridia*), and this long run is closely associated with the site of the Banqueting House, the last surviving room of the Whitehall Palace through which Charles I walked to his execution. It has a fine ceiling painted by Rubens showing his father James I being taken to Heaven by angels, and he stopped and looked up at it before leaving the Palace through a first-floor sash-window to be beheaded on a high scaffold erected in the street outside.

Coronation processions and pageant entertainments

In the early days coronations were celebrated with pageant entertainments rather than masques. These took place in streets during coronation processions. During her coronation procession Elizabeth I was carried through the streets of London from the Tower to Westminster on a golden litter from which she viewed five pageant entertainments in Gracechurch Street; Cornhill; Soper Lane (no longer in existence, but in historical records); Little Conduit in Cheapside; and the Conduit along Fleet Street. This happened on Saturday 14 January 1559, the day before her coronation.

James I's coronation procession passed under seven triumphal archways in the city of London on its way to the Palace at Whitehall and he viewed pageant entertainments under all seven arches: under a Londinium arch at the east end of Fenchurch Street (which focused on the monarchy); an Italian arch in Gracechurch Street (which focused on succession, continuity and unity); a Dutch arch at the Royal Exchange, Cornhill (which focused on foreign policy); an arch above Great Conduit in Cheapside (which showed *Arabia Britannica*); an arch close to Little Conduit, Cheapside (which portrayed peace and bounty); an arch above the Conduit along Fleet Street (which addressed the new world), where the dramatist Thomas Middleton made a speech; and an arch at Temple

Bar, a representation of the Temple of Janus (which portrayed power, peace and wealth). See Michelle Castelletti, *A Picture of Pageantry and the Arches of Triumph*, and its lengthy bibliography of primary and secondary sources.

It is reported that Thomas Dekker wrote pageant entertainments for five of these archways (half the total performance) and that Ben Jonson wrote two (for Fenchurch Street and Temple Bar, the other half of the total performance) – and that as he devised four of the seven archways Ben Jonson preferred to ignore Dekker's contribution in a subsequent book of his two pageant entertainments titled *Part of the King's Entertainment in Passing to his Coronation*.

James I's coronation took place on 25 July 1603, but because of an outbreak of the plague his ceremonial procession through the city of London was postponed until 15 March 1604. (As the new calendar year began on 25 March in England at that time, the procession was originally recorded as happening in 1603.)

The Coronation of King Charles: *a masque with three pageant entertainments*

In this masque on the coronation of King Charles III I have revived the tradition of pageant entertainments, which was last in use in 1661.

This tradition was in operation in 1377 when the 10-year-old Richard II was crowned, and it was in use in the coronations of Elizabeth I and James I as we have just seen, and of Charles I and Charles II (1661). Their pageant entertainments took place on street corners when their coronation processions stopped. James II abandoned the tradition of pageant entertainments to pay for jewels for his Queen, Mary of Modena. A sketch of William III's coronation procession shows the Banqueting House in the background, but by then there were no pageant entertainments. Since then there have been processions at every coronation, but no pageant entertainments. There are three pageant entertainments in *The Coronation of King Charles*.

In *The Coronation of King Charles* I have combined the masque and pageant entertainments. The three pageant entertainments are within a masque form that is traditionally in five sections: prologue; antimasque (a spectacle of disorder and chaos); masque (which transforms the disorder into order and harmony and provides a resolution); revels (which rejoice at the resolution) and epilogue. The three pageant entertainments are in the prologue, antimasque and masque.

The Coronation of King Charles is set in the Banqueting House, and Ben Jonson would recognise the approach of his masques and his pageant entertainments in this work. In *The Coronation of King Charles*

I have moved the pageant entertainments from street corners into the Banqueting House, which was built for James I within the Whitehall Palace to put on masques.

The first pageant entertainment is on King Charles's lineage and refers to the tradition of the Royal Family's descent from the House of David. This descent is traditionally thought to go back to Abraham's grandson Jacob, who dreamed of a ladder that reached to Heaven – while sleeping with his head on a stone pillow believed by many to be the Stone of Scone, the British coronation stone – and of God's covenant and promise that his descendants would rule Israel (*Genesis* 28.11–13, 18). This prophecy was fulfilled by Jacob's descendant David, to whom the covenant was renewed. (In *2 Samuel* 7.12–17, God spoke to Nathan the prophet promising to establish David's dynasty for ever.)

To some this descent is controversial as there is no historical evidence for early Biblical legend. But the tradition is a strong one, and it featured in several publications during Queen Victoria's reign (see p.72). It is an important tradition as the genealogical link (which is set out in full in Appendix 2 on pp.61–72) establishes that the Royal Family are heirs to the Biblical covenant between God and King David's descendants and enjoy the divine right of kings through the Royal Family's successive coronations.

Trilogy and dialectic

With this work I have completed a trilogy of masques.

The first masque, *The Dream of Europa: The Triumph of Peace* (2015), celebrated 70 years of peace in Europe following the disorder of the Second World War.

The second masque, *King Charles the Wise: The Triumph of Universal Peace* (2018), was about the UK's global role after the disorder of Brexit. Minerva, goddess of Wisdom, arranges for the goddesses Britannia, Europa and Columbia (speaking for the UK, Europe and the US respectively) to visit Prince Charles in Buckingham Palace and give their discordant perspectives on the UK's role. The UK's opposition to the EU is presented and a way forward is suggested, through the humanitarian vision of benefiting all humankind by setting up a democratic World State.

The third masque, *The Coronation of King Charles: The Triumph of Universal Harmony*, synthesises the conflicting supranationalistic-European and nationalistic-British themes of the first and second masques in the coming Carolingian Age, in which groundwork will begin for a democratic World State that will bring in an Age of Universal Harmony. This masque contrasts the disorder and chaos of the modern Elizabethan

Age with the order and harmony that will be sought in the coming Age when political Universalism will be prevalent and the prospect of a World State will bring humankind together.

There is a tradition in English literature in which the protagonist wrestles with his soul, as does Dr Faustus when he is visited by Mephistophilis. King Charles also wrestles with his soul in coming to terms with what God and the Prolocutor want his Carolingian Age to achieve.

I said in my Preface to *King Charles the Wise* that in all my works there is a dialectic based on the algebraic formula I found in the East, +A + –A = 0. In the first two masques of the trilogy there is a dialectic between supranationalism (+A, the EU in *The Dream of Europa*) and nationalism (–A, the UK/Brexit in *King Charles the Wise*), which is reconciled in the synthesis of a World State (0, *The Coronation of King Charles*). This masque therefore completes the dialectic between opposites of the other two masques. In each of the three masques there is also a dialectic between disorder and order that is resolved in harmony.

Verse: the tradition of the iambic pentameter with variations as the English heroic line

A word about the verse. For 600 years (1380–1980) from Chaucer to after Tennyson metre was traditional and the iambic pentameter was prominent. It was widespread in Latin as the second line of the elegiac couplet (the first line being a dactylic hexameter), and it has been estimated that three-quarters of English verse written since Chaucer has been in iambic pentameters. Varying the iambic pentameter by including trochees (– ᵕ), anapaests (ᵕ ᵕ –) and dactyls (– ᵕ ᵕ), and other less-well-known feet, allows individual words to be stressed within the regularity of the metre.

When thinking of this tradition in 1779 Dr Johnson wrote of "the music of the English heroic line". In his 'Life of Milton' in *Lives of the Poets* he wrote: "The music of the English heroic line strikes the ear so faintly that it is easily lost, unless all the syllables of every line co-operate together."

Some poets in the 20th century appeared to sweep traditional metre aside in favour of free verse and stress metre, and yet the musical iambic pentameter with variations lurks at the back of apparent irregularity. The opening of Eliot's 'The Waste Land', for example, can be re-lined. The first four lines are in fact three lines of pentameters.

I have stuck with the tradition of the iambic pentameter with variations – indeed, I am one of the few poets, if not the only poet, writing in the 21st century who has continued the tradition in a large body of verse, which puts me treading in the footsteps of the pentameters of Chaucer, Spenser,

Shakespeare, Milton, Marvell, Dryden, Pope, Byron, Keats, Shelley, Wordsworth and Tennyson. The Royal Family spans – and precedes and succeeds – these 600 years, and it is appropriate that a masque celebrating a modern coronation should be in iambic pentameters with variations, an approach that has been in existence in the UK at least since Richard II, who had pageant entertainments at his coronation in 1377. Iambic pentameters with variations have been prominent throughout the British Royal Family's rule since then, and throughout the time of British heraldry since the battle of Agincourt (1415) and the collation by the College of Arms of coats of arms worn on knights' surcoats and shields.

Performance and production
There may seem to be a large cast in the Dramatis Personae, but this masque could be performed by a cast of three (King Charles, Prolocutor/ Minerva, God of the One) and the Chorus of the pageant, who sing all the coronation music. All the live choruses in A within the Dramatis Personae can be drawn from this Chorus, which is present for the whole masque. Some of these live choruses marked † in A within the Dramatis Personae could be filmed prior to the production and be shown on screen so they do not need to be present in the Banqueting House. This would reduce the size of the cast. All the choruses in B within the Dramatis Personae are only on screen and will not be present in the Banqueting House. The size of the cast will depend on how many of the choruses are being put on screen, which will be the Director's decision depending on how lavish the performance of the coronation masque should be.

There are Notes to the Director and the Director of Music on pp.xxi– xxii. I would like the role of Director to be offered in the first instance to Sir Jonathan Bate, who can be contacted via Worcester College, Oxford; and the role of Director of Music to be offered in the first instance to Ian Skelly, who can be contacted via BBC3 where he has presented a music programme, *Essential Classics*, for 20 years. I have spoken with both of them.

Genesis and protocol
I already had the idea for a masque to celebrate the coronation in the autumn of 2015. In a letter to the Prince of Wales on 6 November 2015 (in which I sent him two of my books he had requested, *Selected Poems: Quest for the One* and *Selected Stories: Follies and Vices of the Modern Elizabethan Age*) I wrote:

Having celebrated 70 years of peace in Europe with a masque in the tradition of Ben Jonson's early 17th-century masques, I would like to write a masque on your accession and coronation when the time comes, expressing hopes that a new Carolingian Age will see the solution of many of the world's problems. I glimpsed such a Universal Age in 1983 in 'Night Visions in Charlestown' (Charlestown, the Cornish harbour where I can be found six times a year in what used to be the Harbour-master's house). I have flagged part two of this poem on p.87 [of *Selected Poems: Quest for the One*], and "Charles's town" indicates that more than 30 years ago I associated this new age with your coming reign.

In the same letter I spoke of "the coming Carolingian Age as an era that brings hope to all humankind", an idea that had surfaced as "an Age of Hope", a "Universal Age of Light", in my poem 'Night Visions in Charlestown' (section II of which is titled 'Flight of the Soul to the Coming Age') on 6 August 1983. In a sense in this masque I am delivering (36 years later) a vision I had in August 1983, within a year of writing the first version of my Preface to *Selected Poems: A Metaphysical's Way of Fire* (which was written in September-October 1982).

In a letter of 1 August 2016 to the Prince of Wales I wrote that as King he could "come to be seen as King Charles the Wise", and that "I do seriously intend to put this vision into a masque when I get clear of my immediate duties." *King Charles the Wise* dealt with this and was not linked to his coming coronation. In a letter of 31 July 2017 I wrote that I was preparing to begin this masque (*King Charles the Wise*).

On 30 October 2018 I encountered the Prince of Wales's Assistant Private Secretary, Dr Grahame Davies, at a meeting at the Oxford and Cambridge Club and talked with him privately for 20 minutes. I told him (before giving him a signed copy of my masque *King Charles the Wise*) that I wanted to write a masque that could be performed in the Banqueting House at the time of the coronation. He agreed that as I could see how to do this coronation masque now and would be 80 in May 2019 I should complete the work while I am still *compos mentis* and lodge it with him until the time for a performance is due.

The next day, 31 October 2018, I put this in a letter to him:

I said I would like to write a masque for the coming coronation. I see this as being in the tradition of Ben Jonson's early 17th-century masques, which were performed in the Banqueting House, the successor of the Banqueting Hall in Whitehall, where my masque could be performed. I said that Garter has suggested I should write on this subject to the Lord Chamberlain. You said yesterday a masque was unlikely to be formally commissioned until HRH ascends the throne, and that I could write it now and lodge it with you until that time comes. I propose to do this.

He wrote back that in view of "the sensitivities" protocol would not allow any commissioning. I would have to write this masque on my own initiative and it could be "lodged" until the time came.

In a letter dated 21 November 2018 to Thomas Woodcock, Garter Principal King of Arms, I confirmed the arrangement:

> Last week he wrote to me and said that a masque for the coronation cannot be commissioned at present in view of the sensitivities (of commissioning anything for the coronation before the Queen's demise), but that I can send a masque to him as we had previously arranged. I propose to start this in March, but officially it must be on my own initiative.

In fact, I was delayed by an unexpected invitation to Russia and by the completion of *Fools' Paradise* and *Selected Letters*. I could not make a start until late June 2019, by which time I had mulled over the idea for at least three-and-a-half years.

Russia: 'Vision for Future'

I was invited to Moscow to speak in the semi-governmental Civic Chamber on 22 April 2019, the first day of the new Year of the Phoenix in the Mayan calendar. This only comes round every 2,000 years and is associated with world states, as the audience all knew. The last time it came was shortly after Augustus's reign during the Roman Empire, and with a new World State ahead I was asked to speak for 20 minutes about my *World State* and to launch a new era of universal peace and harmony, which I did. (See my website, Sources, for this speech.) I began by bringing greetings from the UK, "Russia's wartime ally", and I called for better relations between Russia and the West.

I had been asked to bring greetings from Prince Charles, but the Foreign and Commonwealth Office had strict guidelines regarding royal involvement in Russia following the Novichoking in Salisbury, and I was sent a long letter by Sir Alan Duncan, who was in charge of Russia for the FCO, setting out the guidelines I should operate within. I nevertheless received letters from the Office of the Prince of Wales wishing me well on the eve of my departure to Moscow, and sending best wishes shortly after I returned.

At the end of my speech I was awarded a Golden Phoenix by the Russian Ecological Foundation. It was presented by a Russian cosmonaut.

I was also given a silver medal by the BRICS countries (Brazil, Russia, India, China and South Africa) for 'Vision for Future' (the wording on the medal). There were members of the Russian military present, and I was joined on stage by an Admiral and Vice-Admiral, both in full uniform with several rows of ribbon bars, who stood either side of me. Each grasped one of my hands and held it aloft in a victory salute.

My 'vision for future' (to quote my silver medal) was for seeing a united world in my *World State* and *World Constitution*, and for my Universalism (outlined in *The New Philosophy of Universalism*), and the content of my vision must still have been in my mind when I began *The Coronation of King Charles* two months later, on 20 June 2019.

I wrote to the end of the masque section at Connaught House in Essex between then and 24 July, and finished the coronation masque in Charlestown, Cornwall, between 26 July and 3 August 2019.

Banqueting House and Universalist God of the One
On the subject of things still being in my mind, I first visited the Banqueting House in 1966. From 1963 to 1967 I had been living in Japan, where I was a Professor in English Literature at three universities and tutor to Emperor Hirohito's second son, Prince Hitachi, whose State visit to the UK in October 1965 I helped plan. I returned to the UK for a 10-week vacation in 1966 and did extensive literary and historical research while visiting many literary and historical places.

On 8 July I went to the Banqueting House, the only surviving room of the old Whitehall Palace, to walk in Charles I's footsteps and see what he saw on his way to being beheaded on the scaffold outside. I did not then know that I would be able to use this research in my verse play *The Rise of Oliver Cromwell* (2000). The inside of the Banqueting House has been in a deep place in my mind for 53 years, and it is extraordinary – one of the many extraordinary things that have happened in my life – that I should have drawn on those mental images while writing this coronation masque. I would have been amazed to be told then that I would write a masque and pageant entertainments to be performed in the Banqueting House at the time of King Charles III's coronation.

During my time in Japan I became familiar with Buddhism and Taoism, and when I left in 1967 I travelled back through eleven countries and had experience of Hindu India. In 1961–1962 I had lectured in English Literature at the University of Baghdad, Iraq, when Iraq was a backwater that Churchill had created 40 years previously, and I had experience of Islam, which I intensified during my time lecturing at the University of Libya in Tripoli from 1968 to 1970. Throughout that decade I steeped myself in religions other than Christianity and discovered that they all had a common essence in the experience of the mystic Light. I later wrote this up in *The Light of Civilization*. My own experiences of the Light in 1965 and 1971 and subsequently – 93 experiences in all – can be found in my two autobiographical works *My Double Life 1: This Dark Wood* and *My Double Life 2: A Rainbow over the Hills*.

In the 1960s and 1970s I had naturally acquired a Universalist approach to 'God of the One', and saw mystics' experiences in many religions as relating to one God. As I look back again on my visit to the Banqueting House in 1966, it seems perfectly natural to locate God of the One above a balcony in the Banqueting House for the duration of a masque and pageant entertainments.

30 July; 10, 23, 27 August; 5 October 2019

Note to the Director

The first thing to do is to secure agreement to use the venue, the Banqueting House.

The second thing to do is to check through the Dramatis Personae on pp.ix–xii, which lists all the participants in the pageant entertainments, and to think about their groupings within the Chorus of the pageant. Sections of them can speak at different times just as sections are involved in parts of the coronation anthem and other music.

The third thing to do is to work out how stage crew can locate the Light of God of the One on a temporarily-fitted ledge high above the left-hand balcony as you face the throne of the Banqueting House, in the position shown on the front cover, so it shines from high above the balcony down onto the throne.

There will be a large screen above the throne. Speeches can be magnified on the screen for all to see, as happens with political speeches. Thought should be given as to whether any of the early choruses in A within the Dramatis Personae should be pre-recorded and shown on the screen rather than performed live by a chorus stepping forward from the assembled Chorus of the pageant. This would reduce the number in the Chorus of the pageant.

Note to the Director of Music

The first thing to do is to find a living composer whose work approaches the standing of Handel to write the choral music for the anthem and to take account of the stage direction regarding the anthem on pp.5–6. It may be that a dead composer has already written an appropriate piece of choral music to which the words of the anthem can be set.

The second thing to do is to decide on the scale of the production from the musical point of view.

It should be decided whether there will be an organ, full orchestra, string quartet, pianoforte/keyboard, depending on the composition of the choral music for the anthem. There will be a choir positioned on the two side balconies, with scope to sing in antiphonal dialogue at some points. There may be a soloist, or soloists. Please note, the anthem is sung in full on p.6, but is a motif throughout the masque, and there is scope for a soloist to sing part (or parts) of the anthem at later places in the masque.

Different groups within the Chorus of the pageant sing different lines in the anthem and there can be antiphonal dialogue within the swelling choral music. For example, ladies can sing "Let the heavens rejoice" and men can respond "And let the earth be glad" (a heavier line requiring a lower voice). Groups of sopranos, altos, tenors and basses can all be given different lines and all can also sing together in harmony or unison.

The kings and queens and members of the pageant will all need to be choreographed as will the choir.

Note to the Programme Designer

King Charles the Wise should be mentioned in the programme to explain a line like: "I want you to follow up what you've done" (which refers to this earlier masque).

Two views of the inside of the Banqueting House built for James I as a venue for masques, showing the throne, the doors and balconies on either side and the oval painting by Rubens on the ceiling of James I being taken to Heaven by angels. His son Charles I stopped beneath it and looked up before he walked on to an upstairs open sash-window to be beheaded on a high scaffold outside.

THE CORONATION OF KING CHARLES

Prologue

(The Banqueting House, London. A throne at one end with the royal coat of arms, a lion and a unicorn, and high up above the middle of the balcony to the left as shown on the front cover is the Divine Light, which emits a bright glow that cannot be seen through and shines down onto the throne. A screen above the throne stretching between two pillars and not reaching the balconies shows close-ups of the action throughout the masque. Now it shows landmarks of modern London: the Tower, Tower Bridge and Trafalgar Square; and the Houses of Parliament, Westminster Abbey and Buckingham Palace. Cameras. There can be a live stream to screens outside. Through one of the doors on either side of the throne King Charles is carried in on a golden litter, which has met his coach in the course of his procession through London before his coronation. He has stopped off at the Banqueting House to see a pageant entertainment (he has been told), and is following the tradition of Elizabeth I, who was borne in a procession through the streets of London on a golden litter and viewed pageant entertainments the day before her coronation. He dismounts and sits on the throne, spotlit. Behind him through both doors file two lines of kings and queens who head the pageant's coronation procession. A female PROLOCUTOR, spokesperson and narrator, speaks.)

Prolocutor: As a Virgin Mary statue's borne through streets
Lined with applauding crowds during Holy Week,
Queen Elizabeth the First was carried through
London's crowd-lined streets on a golden litter
In a grand royal procession the day before
Her coronation, and viewed five pageant
Entertainments in five of the city's streets
Between the Tower and distant Westminster Hall,
And the crowd's acclaim was part of the ceremony
That installed her as England's new sovereign.
The Virgin Queen transcended her womanhood,
She mesmerised like the eyes on a peacock's tail.
King James the First's grand royal procession
From the Tower through the city to Whitehall
Palace – his home, all round where we are now –

Was postponed because of an outbreak of the plague.
It is good of Your Majesty to agree
To re-enact Elizabeth the First's
Procession and make a ceremonial
Entry on a golden litter to view
The pageant entertainment we shall mount
Here in the Banqueting House your ancestor
King James the First had built, where masques were
    performed,
To mark Your Majesty's coming coronation
Which excites and inspires throughout our land.
I am honoured to be Prolocutor.
And we are sorry that Her Majesty,
Our new Queen, cannot be with you today.
Imagine Your Majesty has just made
A grand royal procession through London's streets
On a golden litter like Elizabeth the First,
And has stopped at this Banqueting House so,
Like the Virgin Queen, you can view a pageant
Entertainment on the dozens of generations
Of your genealogy, that stresses
Your links to all the four much-loved nations
Of the Union that make up the UK.
Its antiquity and universal reach
Show you are a true King of the Union,
A veritable lion with a roar
And a sway that can unify and bring
Peace to large swathes of our great Commonwealth.

(*King Charles stands and bows to the Prolocutor, then
sits. The Prolocutor introduces each king and queen to the
audience.*)

The English royal family's lineage
Can be traced back to the Anglo-Saxon kings
Of Wessex, and to King Alfred the Great,
Ruler of the West Saxons, who declared
Himself king of all the Anglo-Saxons
And unified England against the Danes.

(*Alfred appears and the screen shows film of the partitioning
of England. The royal descent from Alfred is shown on the*

screen. See Appendix 1 for royal descent from Alfred. Each individual king or queen introduced by the Prolocutor steps forward and then steps back. On the screen there is a picture of each king or queen whose name is called. These pictures can be found online at https://www.britroyals.com/royaltree. asp by clicking on the boxed names. Those whose names are spoken after 'via', the non-regal links, are not shown.)

From him came Edward the Elder; Edmund the First;
Edgar the First; Æthelred the Unready;
Edmund the Second; (via Edward the Exile
And Margaret of Scotland) Matilda who
Married Henry the First; and their daughter
Matilda, the Conqueror's granddaughter
Who reigned seven months; Henry the Second;
King John; Henry the Third; Edward the First,
Second and Third; (via John of Gaunt, two Johns
And Margaret Beaufort) Welsh Henry the Seventh;
(Via Margaret Tudor, Scotland's James the Fifth
And Mary Queen of Scots) James the First; (via
Elizabeth of Palatine and Sophia
Of Hanover) George the First and Second; (via
Prince Frederick) George the Third; (via Edward,
Duke of Kent) Victoria; Edward the Seventh;
George the Fifth and Sixth; and Elizabeth
The Second, thirty-second great-granddaughter
Of Alfred – all your forebears hail Your Majesty.

(King Charles stands and bows to the Prolocutor and to his forebears. Close-up of this on the screen. Behind the kings and queens files a pageant representing British society and the multi-racial Commonwealth: representatives of key governing institutions and professions, bodies that work under the monarchy. From their dress can be recognised among them an Archbishop with a mitre, the Speaker of the House of Commons, a judge in a wig, a doctor with a stethoscope, a military leader in uniform, a butcher with an apron, a journalist with a notebook, a TV presenter with a microphone, a labourer with a spade, an old lady with a wicker shopping basket, a Government Minister with a red dispatch-box, a worker in overalls, a soldier in khaki and a road sweeper with a broom. Also can be seen historical figures, including

Solomon, James I, Charles I and Churchill; also Shakespeare, Sir Walter Raleigh, Nelson and Wellington. The pageant arranges itself on either side of the kings and queens before the seated audience and is present throughout the masque. A new coronation anthem plays. A CHORUS OF THE PAGEANT *comprising all kings and queens and members of the pageant sings the coronation anthem, supported by a choir on the two balconies. See the note to the Director of Music on p.xxi for details. The words draw on* 2 Samuel 23.1–4; Isaiah 44.21–23, *and* Psalm 96.11.)

Chorus of
the pageant: David the son of Jesse said,
                   The Spirit of the Lord spake by me
                   And his word was in my tongue.
                   He that ruleth over men must be just,
                   Ruling in the fear of God.
                   And He shall be as the light
                   Of the morning, when the sun riseth,
                   Even a morning without clouds.
                   Let the heavens rejoice,
                   And let the earth be glad.
                   Let the universe rejoice.
                   God save the King, long live the King.
                   Let the universe rejoice.
                   God of the One shall be
                   As the light of the morning.
                   God of the One shall speak
                   Through the Light.

(*Blackout of the pageant. The Light high up above the middle of the balcony to the left brightens as it shines down onto the throne, and from within it* GOD OF THE ONE *speaks exclusively to King Charles, who is enfolded in bright Light. The voice is loud, distant and echoey as if through a loudspeaker. The* CHORUS OF THE PAGEANT, *comprising all kings and queens and members of the pageant, continues singing, mutedly repeating and re-repeating the last four lines of the anthem. They are unaware of the words of God of the One, which they cannot hear.*)

God of the One: I, God of the One, shine my divine Light

Into all souls that open to my Light
In wordless contemplation, just as in
The warm sunlight of a summer's day only
Some flowers open to the sun. I am known
In all cultures through all faiths, I assume
Protean forms: Yahweh, Olympian Zeus,
Jupiter, Allah, Krishna, Buddha, *Tao*.
I shine out through the stars of the Milky Way
And the two hundred billion galaxies
In this part of my expanding universe,
And I shine through the clouds that enfold the earth,
My treasure, for it's only here there's life.
Among all the wastes of my universe,
The barren planets with no atmosphere,
Only the earth has a humankind. It sees
Local differences and local conflicts,
But to me it's a tiny ball that's unified,
To me it's obvious humankind is one
Just as it's obvious to an unschooled pygmy
That an anthill is one society.
I'm proud of the Oneness I have created.
I love the English language, which is known
Throughout humankind, I love all forms of life.
I love green woodpeckers in a fine garden,
And a nuthatch hanging upside down to feed,
And parakeets flitting between oak trees
And jackdaws splashing where a fountain brims.
I love the lilacs and honeysuckle,
And the tinkling goldfinches in thistles.
I love the puffins and the guillemots,
I love corn buntings and fritillaries,
I love the meadow browns and grasshoppers,
I love the sticklebacks and speckled newts,
And the twinkling sunlight in a forest pond.
And I love the badger and the cormorant,
And the whale, the long-time king of the high seas.
I love the viruses and I love the germs,
All microscopic life borne on the wind,
But not pandemics that unbalance my plan.
I love the hornets and the scorpions
And I love the spiders and their silky webs.
Everything that lives in any form is good,

7

Even though it conflicts with other living things
As all are reconciled within harmony.
And I love all humans with a tolerant love,
That is sometimes stretched to nearly breaking-point.
My love is unbounded and immeasurable.
I am well pleased my beloved royal line
In the United Kingdom is being renewed.
I reaffirm the divine right of its kings,
Its God-given and sacred right to rule
Justly, with wisdom and understanding,
And to guarantee democratic freedom
For all British and Commonwealth peoples
And all who live within its territories;
And to support all peoples of the Free World
And work towards the democratic World State
That I long for, when suffering humankind
At last comes of age and pushes aside
Its childish self-interest and cruel wars.
I, Universalist God of humankind,
Shine out for a World State that can bring peace
To all the warring peoples of the earth
So they live together like a swarm of bees
Within a warm garden in summer air
That's redolent with the scents of flowers.
O Charles, Defender of the Anglican Faith,
I, God of the One long known to all the faiths,
God of religious Universalism,
Bring you greetings for your Carolingian Age
Which will restore harmony to the earth.
King Charles, I bathe you in all-embracing Light.

(*The Light floods the throne and then fades and returns to its original brightness. KING CHARLES is still standing before the throne. The pageant is still blacked out. The anthem is still playing softly, with muted singing.*)

King Charles: God of the One and Light, I bow my head
Which will soon be crowned to you, and I promise
And solemnly undertake that I will rule
Justly, with wisdom and understanding.
And I will do all I can to unite
Humankind into one harmonious band

Of brothers and sisters who honour what's good.
Your inspiration feels like a wind from the sea
And I, like a gull hovering hindward, bask
Above the teeming shoals in your plenty.

(KING CHARLES *turns his attention from God of the One
and addresses the pageant. The anthem stops.*)
Let the pageant proceed, this courtly entertainment
Which has shown a lineage from Alfred till now.

(*Lights on the pageant, which comes back to life. The*
PROLOCUTOR *addresses King Charles. The royal descent
from David to James I is shown on the screen. See Appendix
2.*)

Prolocutor: King David, King of Israel, the psalmist,
Was descended from Abraham, and his line
Descends through the kings of Ireland and Argyllshire
And the kings of Scotland and a line in Wales
Through Henry the Seventh – who was descended
From several Welsh royal houses – to James the First,
Who was the hundred-and-tenth in David's line
And ninety-second after King Heremon
Of Ireland and the dilution of Jewish blood.
This line's still party to God's covenants
With Abraham and then David that their
Descendants would be God's chosen people.
This sacred Irish-Scottish-Welsh line binds
The Union of the United Kingdom.
Many may be unaware Your Majesty's
Royal family is the Union's glue.

(*The descent from Abraham to King Charles is shown on the
screen. See Appendix 2.*)

You are God's chosen as the one-hundred-
And-thirty-sixth descendant of Abraham
And the hundred-and-twenty-third of David.
This tree shows that your lineage goes back
To King David, King of Israel, father
Of Solomon, who stands before you now.

(*Solomon steps forward.*)

Here is the Archbishop of Canterbury.

(*The* ARCHBISHOP *speaks. He is wearing his mitre.*)

Archbishop:
Solomon rode upon King David's mule
To Gihon, and Zadok the priest then took
An horn of oil out of the tabernacle,
And anointed him. They blew the trumpet.

(*Solomon has stepped forward with Zadok. Zadok anoints him. This is shown on the screen. A trumpet is blown in accordance with 1 Kings 1.38–40.*)

And all the people said, "God save King Solomon."

Chorus of
the pageant:
God save King Solomon. God save the King.

(*Handel's coronation anthem for the coronation of George II in 1727, which has been sung at all coronations since then, is played; and all sing, including the choir on the two balconies.*)

Zadok the priest
And Nathan the prophet
Anointed Solomon King.
And all the people
Rejoiced, and said:
God save the King!
Long live the King!
May the King live for ever.
Amen, alleluia.

Archbishop:
And at the coronation of Saul, the first
King of Israel whose favourite was David,
All cried in unison "God save the King"
And ever since, in continuity,
The cry has been as now, "God save the King."

Chorus of
the pageant:
God save the King. God save Your Majesty.

(SOLOMON *turns and faces King Charles.*)

Solomon: God save the King.

Prolocutor: God save Your Majesty.

*(Solomon and the Archbishop step back into the pageant.
Spotlight on the PROLOCUTOR. Ben Jonson steps forward.)*

Prolocutor: It is fitting that this celebration,
             This pageant entertainment, should take place
             On the much-written-about site where stood
             The Banqueting Hall of the old Whitehall Palace
             Where masques were once performed for James the
                 First.
             Near here a court entertainment was performed
             For James the First in 1604, some while
             After his coronation, co-written
             By Dekker and Ben Jonson. James saw this
             As his procession passed from the Tower through
                 seven
             Triumphal arches in the City of London.
             Five archways' words were by Dekker, two by
             Jonson (at Fenchurch Street and Temple Bar).
             It is fitting that this celebration,
             This pageant entertainment, should take place
             In this white hall of the old Whitehall Palace,
             In this Palladian hall, this Banqueting House

(Charles I steps forward and re-enacts the scene.)

             Through which King Charles the First walked and
                 looked up
             At the oval Rubens painting of angels
             Taking his father James the First to Heaven,
             Before walking up to the balcony
             And stepping through an open sash-window
             To be beheaded by Cromwell's axeman.
             This celebration purges that dire event.
             Here is Ben Jonson, but first James the First.

(JAMES I *steps forward.*)

James I:

I built this Banqueting House in my Palace
So masques like this could be performed at court.
I am pleased this pageant entertainment
Has been put on for the coronation
Of Your Majesty, my wise descendant.
I watched my son walk under that painting
Of me and trembled with grief at his fate,
And I am pleased that won't happen to you.

(BEN JONSON *points to the screen, which now shows Tudor, pre-Stuart London alongside the Thames and features the Tower. King James I steps forward.*)

Ben Jonson:

The river, running along the city's side,
The Thames, congratulates Your Majesty,
As do Genius, the spirit of this place,
Peace, Wealth; Quiet, Liberty; Safety, great Charles,
And Happiness, who like a settled life
And no Essex rebellion in the streets.
London looks forward to your coming reign
And hopes that it will bring prosperity.

(*The coronation anthem plays; all sing the words, which become muted. Blackout on the pageant. The Light brightens high up above the balcony to the left and shines down onto the Prolocutor.* GOD OF THE ONE *speaks from within the Light to the Prolocutor. Neither King Charles nor the members of the pageant can hear these words.*)

God of the One:

Goddess of Wisdom and daughter of Zeus
(One of my protean forms), wise Minerva,
You who are also Isis and Athena
And implement my wishes down on earth,
You have done well to put yourself forward
In disguise and become Prolocutor
Of this pageant entertainment that instructs.
Just as a wagtail bobs along a wall
And turns and bobs again all the way back
You bob and bob again with useful facts.
I am looking forward to how you portray
The chaos in the UK and the world.
We know the world is in a dreadful state

And that when I sent you down to sound him out
You got Prince Charles to realise he should work
For all humankind. You did brilliantly.
I want you to follow up what you've done.
I'm looking forward to how you portray
King Charles's coming Carolingian Age
And, through this pageant, that I know will reach
A wide viewing audience, stir and wake –
Like an owl swooping at night on a drowsy vole –
The consciousness of dozy humankind
And startle it into wary alertness
So it can see the disorder of this time
And be shocked into enlightened improvement.

(The Prolocutor, who has now been revealed as MINERVA, *speaks to God of the One.)*

Minerva: Lord of all, I've worked hard to do your will
Like a falcon you've sent to hunt from your wrist,
And show King Charles what he's inherited
And his way forward to fulfil your dream.

(The Light fades and returns to its original brightness. The coronation anthem is still being sung, and is no longer muted. The CHORUS OF THE PAGEANT *sings. The volume swells to a crescendo.)*

Chorus of
the pageant: And He shall be as the light
Of the morning, when the sun riseth,
Even a morning without clouds.

(The golden litter is carried in to take King Charles away so the procession can resume. He stands. MINERVA *speaks.)*

Minerva: No, stay. Your Majesty, we have one more
Pageant entertainment for you to watch,
About the world you have inherited,
And the two vices you will need to combat.

(King Charles looks puzzled. He resumes his seat on the throne. The golden litter is carried back out.)

13

Antimasque

(King Charles is sitting on his throne. Dark thunderclouds on the screen as the new pageant entertainment begins. MINERVA, the Prolocutor, speaks.)

Minerva:

In her second pageant entertainment Queen
Elizabeth the First was revealingly
Shown her Government as characterised by
Four virtues – True Protestant Religion,
Love of subjects, and Wisdom and Justice –
Trampling Superstition and Ignorance,
Their two vices. Your Majesty, *your* second
Pageant entertainment will show problems
That must be urgently addressed, the roots
Of the division within your people
Expressed in a cross-section of their views,
And of the confusion over Brexit;
And a crumbling World Order with no rules.
This second pageant entertainment dwells
On two vices: Superstition (deluded
Credulity) and passionate Ignorance
That brought chaos and hard-line division
To the last years of the Elizabethan Age.

(Violent explosions on the screen, the bombing of London in 1940, during the Second World War. The whine of doodle-bugs.)

The Blitz, the Nazis' bombing of London,
Many ruined houses in the East End.
Britain stood alone, still a Great Power,
Against a hostile Europe that wished it ill.
Doodle-bugs, pilotless V-1 rockets,
Flew across the Channel and then cut out –

Homeless
Londoner:

I'd count to ten and hear a bang and know
I was still alive, many were less lucky.

(On the screen, collapsed houses. Damage to Buckingham Palace.)

Minerva: Buckingham Palace was bombed. King George the Sixth
Visited those made homeless in their London streets.

War victim: Seventy million were killed in the Second World War.
Our windows were blown out, I picked up glass.
I knew then as a boy, war just spreads death.

(CHORUS OF THE PAGEANT *speaks. Each line is
spoken by a different voice.*)

Chorus of
the pageant:
  Old lady: Alas, we lost our loved ones and our homes.
  Minister: We beat Hitler, but our Empire tottered.
  Worker: We'd had to borrow to fight, we were skint.
  Journalist: Those were dark days when we lived from day to day.
  Judge: We were free from air attacks but we had nothing.
  Butcher: It was a grim time and hope kept us going.
  Soldier: Labour would build a land fit for heroes.
  Road sweeper: Alas, we worked for a subsistence wage.
  Doctor: We'd have the NHS but little else.

(*On the screen the US nuclear bomb explodes over
Hiroshima. A Russian nuclear test followed by the Berlin
Wall in 1961.*)

Minerva: Soviet expansion. The US. Cold War.
Both sides fought proxy wars in small countries.

(*On the screen a map of the world shows the countries of
the Commonwealth into which most of the British Empire
collapsed. See Appendix 3.*)

A wind of change brought decolonising,
Europe's empires broke up, colonies were freed.
The British Empire crumbled after Suez
And then collapsed into the Commonwealth,
Which had just eight countries when the Queen was
    crowned.

(*The European Common Market is on the screen.*)

Trying not to turn its back on the Commonwealth,
The UK joined the European Common Market
For the world power that membership would bestow.

(*The screen shows in quick succession iconic scenes of
Vietnam, the Berlin Wall, 9/11, Afghanistan, Ukraine,
Crimea and Syria.*)

Since then the West has endured continual wars.
Vietnam was lost, Western leaders held firm.
The Berlin Wall fell, then the Soviet Union.
The Middle East seethed with new turbulence.
After nine-eleven the West fought factions within
Islam in Afghanistan and Iraq.
It seemed the West had won but the Russian
Federation sought to restore the Soviet Empire.
It intervened in Ukraine and annexed Crimea
And fought the West in Syria and dislodged
Millions of refugees to flood Europe.

(*On the screen, a list of 162 wars.*[1])

Since the Second World War the UN has failed
To prevent a hundred-and-sixty-two
Further wars, it's been a most troubled time.
So many families lost relatives
In these wars of attrition and decline.

(*The screen shows a list of 72 wars.*[2])

Minerva: Right now seventy-two wars are still being fought
Which the UN is unable to prevent.
And there are thirteen thousand nine hundred
Nuclear weapons, and a terrorist may steal one.

(*The screen shows a map of the world and the locations of
these nuclear weapons. They headline the total number of
nuclear weapons. The figure can be updated to the total at
the time of the coronation.*)

The world's in chaos, the Cold-War rules have gone.
The Commonwealth now has fifty-four countries.

The European Union and its earlier forms
Have kept the peace since nineteen-forty-five,
But a United States of Europe's ahead
And after eight years of austerity
The UK voted to leave, and was divided.
Some hoped leaving would turn the Commonwealth
(Which has 2.4 billion citizens)
Into a central influence in the world
And restore the UK's wartime standing
When it stood alone with its own sovereignty.
Some thought leaving would make the UK richer.
Some thought it would make the UK poorer
And marginalise it on the world scene.
The outlook was uncertain and there were still
Seventy-two wars the UN could not stop.
The UK seemed to be in a great mess,
There was disorder, all longed for order.
Then Covid came, and ruinous lockdowns,
Catastrophic borrowing that will blight decades
And the biggest hit to the economy
Since the Great Frost of 1709.
This, Your Majesty, is the world that you
Have inherited from the previous Age,
A world that's overlooked poor humankind.
Angry Brexiteers want to petition you.
Some are snorting like bulls about to charge
And some are like honking and squawking geese.

(*A* CHORUS OF ANGRY BREXITEERS *steps forward from the pageant. Each line is spoken by a different Brexiteer. This brings out their conflicting views and suggests a complete mess. The Brexiteers are a mixture of blimpish elderly figures looking back to the UK of their childhood and seeking to revive the UK's stature at the end of the First World War, and upwardly-mobile, ill-educated, self-assertive, middle-aged English who speak with demotic and regional accents and do not like immigrants.*)

Chorus of
angry
Brexiteers: We are all angry, furious Brexiteers.
                Your Majesty, we are fuming with rage.

The referendum result was to leave.
But Remainers in the Government delayed.
It was an insult to democracy.
They're weasels, none of them can be trusted.
No one voted for 'no deal', just to leave.
Leaving with 'no deal'? An act of self-harm.
The EU's the UK's biggest market.
We'd have lost a huge chunk of our trade and jobs.
Scotland and Wales would break, Ireland unite.
We needed to leave or the Tory Party was dead.
We needed to stay to keep food on the shelves.
Like the Roman Empire the EU's built roads,
And given us clean air and clean beaches.
It's like the Reformation, we hate Europe.
The EU's like the Pope, we're better out.
A United States of Europe's the way forward.
We can all unite behind a hard Brexit.
We love all British subjects with low tax.
We'll have wise policies for social justice.
We're fuming with anger as it's all too slow.
We want to unite for a global destiny.
What global role for the UK in your new Age?

Minerva: Now indignant historical figures
            Much troubled by the roles of the UK,
            Europe and the US express concern.

            (*A* CHORUS OF INDIGNANT HISTORICAL
            FIGURES *steps forward:* HENRY VIII, SHAKESPEARE,
            DRAKE, SIR WALTER RALEIGH, JAMES I, NELSON,
            WELLINGTON, EARL HAIG *and* CHURCHILL.)

Chorus of
indignant
historical
figures: We are indignant historical figures
            And we are appalled at the loss of direction.
            For centuries the UK has stood alone –
            But has at the same time always been part
            Of European civilisation,
            Engaged with the Continent in many wars,
            Involved with Catholics and Protestants,

19

And had America as a colony.
And today which way does the UK look:
Inward to itself, outward to Europe
Or further outward to America
Which English ships planted and speaks English?
It's not clear if the UK's destiny's
Britain alone, with Europe or the US.

Minerva: The British poor wait to petition you.
Some scavenge for food like foxes round bins.

(*A* CHORUS OF THE BRITISH POOR *steps forward.*
Lines are spoken by different poor people. The Chorus is
drawn from British society and comprises the modern poor:
a homeless man, a nurse, a healthcare worker, a teaching
assistant, a police officer, a retired soldier and a pensioner.)

Chorus of the
British poor: We are the badly-treated British poor,
We are downtrodden, filled with hopelessness.
Some of us are homeless, and some have homes
But can't make ends meet and we need food banks.
We can't find jobs in once-thriving London,
And those of us in work can't afford food,
Including nurses, healthcare workers, police
Officers, part-time teachers and retired soldiers
Who fought for this country and now sleep in doorways.
Some of us are on zero-hours contracts,
Some weeks we work zero hours for zero pay.
Every day we despair, we're in misery.
We sit near lavender and a song thrush sings,
We watch a robin hop onto a spade.
Please give us roofs over our heads after
Your coronation. We are in chaos
And long for order and enough to eat.

Minerva: And here are the wretched of the Commonwealth.
Some sit listlessly like cows in a field.

(*A* CHORUS OF THE WRETCHED OF THE
COMMONWEALTH *steps forward. Lines are spoken by*
different wretched people. The Chorus is drawn from the

Commonwealth nations and comprises a wretched South African, Kenyan, Pakistani, Canadian, Jamaican, Cypriot and New Zealander.)

Chorus of the
wretched of the
Commonwealth: We are the wretched of the Commonwealth.
We have been overlooked by the governments
Of the nation-states in which we reside.
We are the forgotten, we don't feature
In what our states consider should be done.
We lollop like rabbits but go nowhere.
We sit among cobwebs and watch spiders.
We long for racial harmony and homes,
And funding that will guard our communities
So we can live peaceful and prosperous lives.
Please help us, Your Majesty, please give us
Shelter from the hot sun and monsoon rains.
We look to you as Head of the Commonwealth.
We know you care, please see that we are fed.

Minerva: And suffering humankind pleads with you.
Some crouch like mangy dogs amid ruins.

(A CHORUS OF SUFFERING HUMANKIND steps forward. Lines are spoken by different suffering people. The Chorus is drawn from every continent and comprises a suffering American, European, African, Middle Eastern, Indian, Australian, Russian and Chinese.)

Chorus of
suffering
humankind: We are suffering humankind, we squat
Amid wars in ruins and in hovels.
We have bare feet and live in long nightshirts.
We are blasted by rockets and chew our cheeks.
We beg but our bowls are usually empty.
We forage on rubbish dumps and in bins.
We look for pear trees and gooseberry bushes.
We dream we keep chickens and a donkey.
We endure every medical condition.
Famine, disease and poverty are rife.

The seasons bring extremes of drought and floods.
We are exposed to what our climate's changed.
We can't find work, we have large families.
Our children are hungry and don't know school.
We are cold at night and we sit in the shade
During the heat and conserve our energy.
Life is a daily struggle, an ordeal.
We do our best for our families but they starve.

Minerva: Your Majesty, this pageant entertainment
Has drawn your attention to the two vices
That are responsible for the disorder
You have inherited from the previous Age:
Superstition, deluded credulity,
The belief that the UK can stand alone,
Strong in British Exceptionalism,
With hardly any Navy and not enough
Income from trade to run its Welfare State
Without help from Europe, that's now rallying
Into a United States of Europe,
Or from the United States of America;
And Ignorance, that leads a nation-state
Into a credulity that creates chaos
And disorder through lack of a clear role.

(KING CHARLES *stands and addresses Minerva.*)

King Charles: This second pageant entertainment has been
More political than the first one on my lineage.
This one has been on the discord in the world.
I am concerned for the poor and the wretched,
And the suffering on all parts of the earth.
I try to keep political thinking
Separate from what the monarchy will do
Just as stables should be separate from a House.
And yet I am Head of the Commonwealth
Of nation-states, once in the British Empire,
And I want them to be free from the scourge of war,
Of poverty and poor infrastructure,
Of homelessness, hunger and chronic want,
And I am aware my coming Age should solve
All these problems, and end all division,

Stop all the wars, and to this disorder
Bring order and new hope and harmony
To the long-suffering well-wishing peoples
Of the UK, Commonwealth and humankind.

(*King Charles signals for his golden litter to be brought.
The golden litter is carried in to take King Charles away but
MINERVA holds up her right hand and speaks.*)

Minerva: No, stay. Your Majesty, we have one more
Pageant entertainment for you to watch,
About the coming Carolingian Age
That you will preside over and help to shape,
And the four virtues you'll need to do this.

(*King Charles again looks puzzled. He resumes his seat on
the throne. The golden litter is carried back out.*)

Masque

(Immediately afterwards. MINERVA *addresses King Charles.)*

Minerva:
Now may it please Your Majesty to view –
Here where your ancestor King James viewed masques
Before he was taken to Heaven by angels
As painted above us by the great Rubens –
One more pageant entertainment which reveals
The *Zeitgeist* of your Carolingian Age,
A looking-outwards and a global reach
That will embrace the Commonwealth nations
With an internationalist perspective
And will be hailed among all nation-states
As the birth of a Universalist Age.
Your Majesty, thanks to your influence
And your encouragement of the Commonwealth
The international community will seek
To explore a new world structure that will fill
All humankind with harmony and hope.
This third pageant entertainment shows you
Characterised by four virtues – a true view
Of Britain; love of your subjects, the poor and wretched;
Wisdom towards suffering humankind;
And Justice in bringing in a new world
That will solve inequality and want.
Let's look ahead and approach the coming Age
Through the people who have already spoken
In dissatisfaction but are now satisfied,
Who speak from the future deep into your reign,
Starting with the once-angry Brexiteers.

(The CHORUS OF ANGRY BREXITEERS *steps forward.)*

Chorus of angry
Brexiteers:
Your Majesty, we once-angry Brexiteers
Thank you for standing up for harmony.
We know you've steered the country into calm.
Everything is good in our country now.
We've moved beyond Brexit, which is in the past.
We've moved beyond battling over in and out.

We are now part of a new-won Britain
That's confident in its values and is admired
Throughout the world. We are ourselves again.
We all feel we are still Europeans
For our people all came from Europe: Celts,
Romans, Angles, Saxons, Jutes, Vikings, Danes,
Normans, Belgians, Dutch, Germans, all races.
And we all have a shared history, we all
Share the Pope and the Protestants' reforms,
Napoleon, Fascists and Communists.
We stood up to tyranny and are free,
And what we stand for's clear to all the world.
We believe the UK is Paradise.

Minerva:

Now once-indignant historical figures
Who were much exercised by the conflict between
The UK, Europe and America.

(*The* CHORUS OF INDIGNANT HISTORICAL
FIGURES *steps forward.*)

Chorus of
indignant
historical
figures:

We once-indignant historical figures
Thank you for redefining the UK's role.
Traditionally, the UK's stood between
Three circles: Empire and the Commonwealth;
America's special relationship;
And Europe, now "ever-closer union".
The UK had a choice, its destiny
Could be with the EU or the US –
The world of Old Europe or the New World –
Or to stand alone as Britannia of old.
Some said standing alone would be folly:
Imperial nostalgia and leadership
Of the global Commonwealth weren't feasible,
Britannia'd be an insignificant,
Inward-looking and irrelevant island
With no great influence on world affairs –
And as a manufacturing, trading nation
Lacking mineral or agricultural

Resources, or military strength, should be
Siding with both the EU and US
At the same time, and be a bridge for them.
Some said Britannia'd be a satellite
Invested in and protected by the US –
Some said the UK'd be to the US
As the Channel Islands have been to the UK.
Some said the UK should not be a vassal state,
And should have a trade and foreign policy
That suits an independent nation-state.
We're pleased this dilemma has been resolved.
We're satisfied with the way things have turned out.
We thank you for urging being aligned
To a new Universalist Union.
We historical figures applaud you
And hail a UK that looks to humankind
And a new world structure that we approve.

Minerva: And here are the British poor you have helped.

(*The* CHORUS OF THE BRITISH POOR *steps forward.*)

Chorus of the
British poor: Your Majesty, we British poor thank you.
We know you've told politicians to change
The way we are treated. They've cleared the streets,
We all have roots, many of us have found work.
No one starves now, there's a more caring feel
About officialdom, they want to help.
We know from speeches you have made that you
Are on our side and want us to partake
Of the new money our global outlook
Has brought into the Government's coffers.

Minerva: And here are the wretched of the Commonwealth,
More hopeful now than they have ever been.

(*The* CHORUS OF THE WRETCHED OF THE
COMMONWEALTH *steps forward.*)

Chorus of the
wretched of the
Commonwealth: We wretched of the Commonwealth thank you.
We know you have spoken with our leaders
And urged that we should now be looked after,
Given homes in crime-free communities,
And lifted out of our old wretched lives.
We know you have called for more investment
So our living conditions can improve.
We know you want us all to be well-fed.
We thank you for caring for all of us.

Minerva: And finally, suffering humankind.

(*The* CHORUS OF SUFFERING HUMANKIND *steps forward.*)

Chorus of
suffering
humankind: We who were suffering humankind thank you.
We know you have spoken with the UN
Secretary-General and with Presidents.
You've tried to protect us from the ravages of war.
We know you've asked for us to be fed and housed,
You've pleaded with our leaders to clear us
From ruins and look after our families,
Send our children to school and give us peace.
We live in the harmony of your support.
We know you care for us, we know you want
Leaders to bring in a new world structure.
We thank you for your concern for humankind.

Minerva: Your Majesty, they all speak well of you,
Angry Brexiteers, the poor, the wretched
Of the Commonwealth and suffering humankind.
All are as contented as grazing sheep
And horses munching near a blackberry hedge.
All recognise the influence you'll assert.

(MINERVA *now speaks directly to King Charles. Both are spotlit. Blackout on the pageant. Only King Charles hears her words.*)

"You will be a King with higher consciousness
And a clear mind who'll speak for humankind."
You've heard those words before, do you know when?

(KING CHARLES *speaks. Only Minerva hears his reply.*)

King Charles: Minerva. I…. I recognise you now.
I still think of you as an Athenian owl.
You showed me all the post-Brexit options.
You came to me as Goddess of Wisdom
And ended crowning me King Charles the Wise.

Minerva: I did. And I need you to be wise now.
Now our pageant entertainment takes a turn
And lifts the curtain drawn across the future
As if this were Apollo's oracle.
Listen carefully to what you're about to hear.

(*The spotlights fade, lights back on the pageant.* MINERVA *speaks to him as Prolocutor.*)

Your Majesty, your reign will restore order.
Look at the screen, for you will catch glimpses
Of what you'll seek to bring in, your progress
Towards a coalition of nations
Who can work together in harmony.

(*Blackout on the pageant. The screens show King Charles addressing the Commonwealth leaders.* MINERVA *speaks to King Charles. Both are spotlit. The pageant cannot hear.*)

You're seeking to unify the Commonwealth
As a stepping-stone towards a greater goal
That you have had in mind, and the groundwork
For this goal will be achieved in your reign
Even though the end-result is more distant.
The Carolingian Age will point the way.
The new world structure belongs to a later reign.

(*The screen shows the UN General Assembly.*)

Listen to what the UN delegates say

From a future time about the work you'll do.

(*On the screen a* CHORUS OF UN DELEGATES *drawn from all continents. They include a North American, a South American, a European, an Indian, an African, an Australian, a Russian and a Chinese.*)

Chorus of UN
delegates:

We UN delegates applaud the work
That took place in the Carolingian Age
To seek agreement to abolish war
And end the self-assertion of nation-states
That led to conflicts on every continent
Though cosmonauts had seen the earth as one;
And to enforce disarmament and impound
All the nuclear weapons on the planet.
We applaud the work that took place in your Age
To combat famine, disease and poverty
And solve all environmental problems
And propose central funding for all want.
We applaud the Carolingian Age
Which saw that nation-states required a new
World structure for universal harmony.
We salute your efforts and far-sightedness.
Without them our new world would not be here.

(MINERVA *speaks.*)

Minerva:

Now listen to the Representatives
And Senators of the democratic World State
Who speak from an even more distant time.

(*The Chorus of UN delegates fades from the screen and is replaced by a chart captioned 'Diagram/Flow Chart of the Supranational Authority: The Structure of the World State'.*[3] *Beneath it from the distant future stand the* CHORUS OF REPRESENTATIVES AND SENATORS OF THE DEMOCRATIC WORLD STATE.)

Chorus of
Representatives
and Senators of
the democratic
World State:

We Representatives and Senators
Of the democratic World State salute you.
We now govern the world from our HQ
Which has just enough authority to see
That, thanks to our World Army, war's no more,
And that, thanks to our brilliant negotiators,
Nuclear weapons have now ceased to exist.
We live in an Age where want has been abolished.
There is no hunger, there is no illness,
All humankind has sufficient to live
In comfort. Poverty is of the past.
All this began in the Carolingian reign
Which gave prominence to thinking before then.
From our Age of Universal Harmony
We salute you for your vision which brought us in.
We applaud your influence on looking beyond
Coalitions of nation-states to this,
Our unified, democratic World State.

(*The Chorus of Representatives and Senators of the
democratic World State points to the chart above them.
MINERVA speaks to King Charles, who is spotlit. The
pageant is still blacked out.*)

Minerva:

Your Majesty, this pageant entertainment
Has drawn your attention to the four virtues
That will create your Carolingian Age:
A true and lucid view of the UK
As standing alone but aligned with a growing power;
Love of all your subjects, including the poor
And wretched; Wisdom, which empathises
With suffering humankind beyond all borders;
And Justice, which creates an equal world
With a new democratic structure for humankind.
Four virtues Your Majesty shows in abundance.
Your Majesty, how do you react to that?

King Charles:

I am amazed. It's what I have sometimes thought

And secretly hoped for in my wildest dreams
But never expected could possibly happen.
I am King of the United Kingdom
Of four nations and many territories
And I am also Head of the Commonwealth.
Ever since Garter stood on the balcony
(The Proclamation Gallery above Friary Court)
At St James's Palace and proclaimed me King,

(*On the screen is a picture of the 1952 proclamation on
the balcony of St James's Palace, showing 21 people on
the balcony; and in another picture the Garter Principal
King of Arms with the Earl Marshal and Clarenceux and
Norroy and Ulster Kings of Arms. A re-enactment of the
proclamation of the reign of King Charles now shows the
contemporary Garter Principal King of Arms in a bicorn
hat on a balcony, miming. Beside him in the shadows
are four heralds, all in gold tunics as Garter mouths the
proclamation. This replaces the 1952 proclamation on
screen.*)

I have been thinking how global Britain
Can use Government assets to extend
Its global standing and relationships
And champion the rules-based international
Order so the UK is more open,
Outward-looking and confident in the world.
I have been thinking about the linking
Of Free-World democracies – the Commonwealth
Provides many links – and common values.
The internationalism of past years
Did not sit well with Brexiteers' 'UK First'
And their denouncing of globalism.
I've been thinking like a sawing grasshopper:
'Global Britain' seems a hollow promise.
But now I see again what you helped me see:
That though it will take time, the work starts now,
And I'll engage with UN delegates,
For beyond them are the Representatives
And Senators of the democratic World State
That has long been the dream of all humankind
And is the goal of all who would bring in

A universal peace and harmony.
I must get the Commonwealth hosting world leaders,
I must talk political Universalism
With the world figures I meet and the UN.
I would like London to be the centre
Of a new world order that can broker peace.
The Carolingian Age must lay groundwork
For the Age of Universal Harmony
The Representatives and Senators
Were speaking from. I will use my influence
Like a squirrel gathering and storing nuts.

(The pageant is still in blackout. Now GOD OF THE ONE
*shines brilliant Light on King Charles and on Minerva from
high up above the balcony to the left, and speaks.)*

God of the One: I, God of the One, have listened and am well pleased.
The Carolingian Age will be transitional.
It will take humankind from its aggressive warring
To the seat of its soul where spiritual harmony reigns,
And will leave it better off although the work
Will not be finished in your lifetime, King Charles.
Minerva, you have put on an excellent show.
Your pageant entertainment has revealed
The coming Age, has raised the curtain and peeped
Into the future and the perfect world
I dream of, to which humans have been blind.

Minerva: Lord of all, thank you. I'm pleased to do your will.

*(The spotlights fade, lights back on the pageant. On the
screen is* KING CHARLES *speaking lines near the end of
his speech.)*

King Charles: A universal peace and harmony.
I must get the Commonwealth hosting world leaders,
I must talk political Universalism
With the world figures I meet and the UN.
I would like London to be the centre
Of a new world order that can broker peace.
The Carolingian Age must lay groundwork
For the Age of Universal Harmony.

*(The pageant has not heard anything since the sixth line of
Minerva's speech after the Chorus of suffering humankind,
which mentions "the influence you'll assert". All in the
pageant now applaud.)*

Minerva: Elizabeth the First viewed five pageant
            Entertainments and James the First viewed seven
            Along their coronation processions,
            But we are of the view that three's enough
            In this Banqueting House, and our pageant
                entertainments
            Must be performed within a masque's structure.
            We've had the Prologue and the Antimasque's
            Disorder, and we have now had the Masque.
            Order has been restored. Now for the Revels.

(All cheer "Hooray".)

Revels

(Immediately afterwards. On the screen, King Charles sits on the coronation chair in Westminster Abbey. MINERVA *addresses King Charles, standing before the pageant.)*

Minerva:

And now our pageant shows the rejoicing
At the coming of the Carolingian Age
And revels in the music that was heard
In all the coronations since Edgar
Who was crowned in Bath Abbey in 973,
In the long tradition since the Anglo-Saxons
Of which Your Majesty is now a part.
But first once more the choral anthem for
Your coronation, which we hear again.

(On the screen is a succession of historical images of the coronations of Kings as they are mentioned, starting with another image of King Charles in Westminster Abbey. The CHORUS OF THE PAGEANT *sing the coronation anthem again. The mood is one of rejoicing, and among the members of the pageant there is some celebratory dancing.)*

Chorus of
the pageant:

David the son of Jesse said,
The Spirit of the Lord spake by me
And his word was in my tongue.
He that ruleth over men must be just,
Ruling in the fear of God.
And He shall be as the light
Of the morning, when the sun riseth,
Even a morning without clouds.
Let the heavens rejoice,
And let the earth be glad.
Let the universe rejoice.
God save the King, long live the King.
Let the universe rejoice.
God of the One shall be
As the light of the morning.
God of the One shall speak
Through the Light.

Minerva:	Now 'Zadok the Priest', sung at all English Coronations since King Edgar's in Bath Abbey in 973 and for James the First; Set by Tomkins for Charles the First and set By Lawes for Charles the Second's coronation; And in Handel's setting sung at all English Coronations since King George the Second.

(*The* CHORUS OF THE PAGEANT *sing Handel's version of 'Zadok the Priest'. The screen shows historical images of Edgar, James I, Charles I, Charles II and George II.*)

Chorus of the pageant:	Zadok the priest And Nathan the prophet Anointed Solomon King. And all the people Rejoiced, and said: God save the King! Long live the King! May the King live for ever. Amen, alleluia.

Minerva:	Now 'I was glad' set by Pigott for Queen Anne; by Attwood for George the Fourth; and by Parry for Edward the Seventh. Then Croft's 'The Lord is a sun and a shield' for George the First.

(*The* CHORUS OF THE PAGEANT *sing extracts from these pieces of music. The screen shows historical images of Queen Anne, George IV, Edward VII and George I.*)

Now extracts from Handel's 'Let thy hand be Strengthened', 'The King shall rejoice' and 'My heart Is inditing', sung at King George the Second's Coronation, and at many crownings since.

(*The* CHORUS OF THE PAGEANT *sing these extracts. The screen shows a historical image of George II.*)

Now Attwood's 'O Lord, grant the King a long life' For William the Fourth, and Knyvett's 'This is

The day that the Lord hath made' for Victoria.

(*The* CHORUS OF THE PAGEANT *sing extracts from these pieces of music. The screen shows historical images of William IV and Victoria.*)

Now Bridge's 'Kings shall see and arise' for
Edward the Seventh, and Elgar's 'O hearken
Thou' for George the Fifth, followed by Davies'
'*Confortare* (Be strong and play the man)'
For George the Sixth, three twentieth-century extracts.

(*The* CHORUS OF THE PAGEANT *sing extracts from these pieces of music. The screen shows historical images of Edward VII, George V and George VI.*)

And now Vaughan Williams' 'Festival *Te Deum*'
For George the Sixth, and his 'O taste and see'
For our much-loved Elizabeth the Second.

(*The* CHORUS OF THE PAGEANT *sing extracts from these pieces of music. The screen shows historical images of George VI and Elizabeth II.*)

And finally Howell's 'Behold O God
Our defender', Walton's 'Coronation
Te Deum' and Willan's 'O Lord our Governour'
Also for Elizabeth the Second.

(*The* CHORUS OF THE PAGEANT *sing extracts from these pieces of music. The screen shows a historical image of Elizabeth II.* MINERVA *addresses King Charles.*)

Your Majesty, we revellers applaud
Your succession to this musical tradition.

(*The* CHORUS OF THE PAGEANT *applaud King Charles, who stands from the throne, bows and then sits.*)

But now historical figures revel,
Thrilled at your impending coronation
And thrilled at the coming Carolingian Age.

They reveal their delight at its prospects.
Many would speak with you to express their joy.
But first your ancestor King James the First –
Who viewed seventeenth-century masques in this very
    hall
And is still shy of speaking like the Duke
In *Measure for Measure* Shakespeare based on him –
Wishes to embrace you for what you will do.

(*King Charles rises from the throne and stands. James I
advances to the throne and embraces him warmly. Shakespeare
has also advanced and is by his side. He bows respectfully.
King Charles enthusiastically shakes his hand. Ben Jonson
advances and also bows. King Charles shakes his hand. The
members of the pageant applaud. There is a brief chant.*)

Chorus of
the pageant: Shakespeare, Shakespeare, Shakespeare. Jonson,
Jonson.

(*King Charles sits on the throne.*)

Minerva: Here are the shades of nine Kings and leaders.

(*On the screen appears a* CHORUS OF SHADES OF
NINE KINGS AND LEADERS: ALFRED, HAROLD II,
WILLIAM THE CONQUEROR, HENRY II, HENRY
VIII, GEORGE III, PALMERSTON, CHURCHILL
and KEIR HARDIE, *each named on screen in subtitles.
Members of the pageant look up at the screen. Some point.*)

Chorus of nine
Kings and
leaders: We, historical Kings and past leaders,
All want global Britain to lead again,
To show the world the way forward after
A time of long decline from what it was.
But it's the fifth-largest economy
Still, and the fifth-largest military power
In the world after the US, Russia,
China and India and now has vision.
We see beyond nation-states and endorse

The work the Carolingian Age will start
To bring all humankind together in
A World State that will solve all the problems.
We're overjoyed at the prospect of what
You'll do to influence a new direction
And bring in a new Golden Age of peace
In which, in place of wars and nuclear
Weapons, there's universal harmony.

Minerva: And here are well-known historical leaders
. From the British Empire and Commonwealth.

(On the screen appears a CHORUS OF HISTORICAL
LEADERS FROM THE BRITISH EMPIRE AND
COMMONWEALTH, *all now dead. Gandhi, Nehru and
Nkrumah can be seen. Again there is nudging and pointing
among members of the pageant.)*

Chorus of leaders
from the British
Empire and
Commonwealth: We leaders from the past British Empire
And Commonwealth rejoice that the UK
Will start work on linking all nation-states
And leading them towards a new World State
That will come up with central solutions
To the world's famine, disease, poverty,
Global warming and climate change. We hope
Your Majesty will influence this research
And urge that a consensus should be found
To make this change during the coming Age,
Your Carolingian Age we all await,
The Age of Harmony we all long for.

Minerva: And now the British people want to speak.
(On the screen, a CHORUS OF BRITISH PEOPLE *in the
future, all classes and professions, some in suits and some
casually dressed.)*

Chorus of
British people: We, the British people, are delighted
That your Carolingian Age will bring

New influence in the world, so our UK
Becomes a global power again and steers
All humankind towards a new World State.
We hope Your Majesty will influence
The world leaders into taking on board
The new world structure, which will begin in
The research you will promote as our King.
We've been the most inventive nation-state
And we have shared our inventions with the world,
And we are still inventing, have more to give.
We hear the cuckoo in a distant copse,
We are optimistic as we pioneer
To bring in a new Golden Age of peace,
A new harmony to unite humankind.

Minerva: And look at the world's united peoples.

(*On the screen a* CHORUS OF THE WORLD'S UNITED
PEOPLES *in the future. Men, women and children of every
nationality and colour. Some lines are spoken by individuals
within the Chorus.*)

Chorus of the
world's united
peoples: We, the world's united peoples, are pleased
To greet you before your coronation.
We know that work began during your reign
To do the research that brought our federal
World State into existence. We applaud
The initiative of the Carolingian Age
That laid the groundwork for all humankind
To come together in prosperity
And live in peace with sufficient for all.
We rejoice in your reign, which will begin
The Golden Age humankind now enjoys.

Minerva: The once-suffering peoples too rejoice.

(*On the screen appears a* CHORUS OF ONCE-
SUFFERING PEOPLES. *Some faces were seen in the
Chorus of suffering humankind. Some lines are spoken by
individuals within the Chorus.*)

Chorus of once-suffering peoples:	We, the once-suffering peoples, rejoice. Thanks to work begun in your reign we now Have hope. We no more shelter in ruins, We are no longer bombed and dyed with blood, We've ceased to be refugees from war zones In the Middle East or from workless Africa. We live normal lives, we have sufficient. And so we hail the Carolingian Age As a turning-point in our bleak fortunes, We're all contented now, no one will starve. The earth is now for us a Paradise.
Minerva:	Here are the eight distinguished supporters Of a new World State from the Cold-War time. (*On the screen appears the* CHORUS OF EIGHT DISTINGUISHED SUPPORTERS *of a new World* *State:* TRUMAN, EISENHOWER, EINSTEIN, CHURCHILL, RUSSELL, GANDHI, J.F. KENNEDY *and* GORBACHEV.)
Chorus of eight distinguished supporters:	We eight supporters of a new World State Are pleased that the Carolingian Age Will work to move on from the nation-state To a new world structure that will include All humankind in one federal harmony, And that through your influence work will start During your reign to progress towards peace, To abolish war and nuclear weapons And make the earth a safer, secure place. No more blots on the earth like Syria. No more ruinous air strikes on the poor. We applaud what research your Age can do To get the world beyond the nation-state And competitive, self-assertive war.
Minerva:	And it's time for a celebratory dance As all the classes of the British here

41

Now dance with each other on equal terms:
Rich man and homeless, judge and prisoner,
Old King and pauper, doctor and diseased,
Minister and labourer, shopkeeper
And shoplifter, policeman and robber,
Angry Brexiteer and bright Remainer:
Tiger and lamb cavorting together,
All opposites reconciled and at one
Within an underlying harmony.

(*The coronation anthem plays 'David the son of Jesse said'.
All members of the pageant dance; where possible opposites
dance together.* KING CHARLES *stands, spotlit, and
addresses the pageant.*)

King Charles: I thank each one of you for performing
These amazing pageant entertainments
About the coming Carolingian Age
So professionally and with such exquisite charm.

(KING CHARLES *turns to Minerva, who is spotlit, and
addresses her with ironical emphasis as 'Prolocutor' and not
'Minerva'.*)

And I thank you, Prolocutor, for acting
As Mistress of Ceremonies, for narrating
The pageant entertainments and introducing
The choruses with such effortless skill
And the elegance of a graceful roe-deer.

(*The members of the pageant applaud. Blackout on the
pageant.* MINERVA *speaks to King Charles. The pageant
cannot hear her words.*)

Minerva: The spirits of the dead have left the screen
And returned to their abode in the Underworld.
But they've left their tribute to Your Majesty.
Our revels have ended but now you know
How the Carolingian Age will be remembered
And what you have to do – who to influence –
To do the groundwork for a new World State
That will resolve the problems of the earth

And bring harmony to all humankind.
You are now like a stag hidden in thickets
But the time will come when your work will be open
And you'll stand like the Monarch of the Glen.
God of the One has sent me down to you
To reveal what the Carolingian Age
Will be remembered for, and now I must
Report on these pageant entertainments
For my work is now done, I must retire.
Farewell, King Charles the Wise, and may you be
Uplifted by your coronation and by
The Light that in a covenant bestows
The divine right of Kings to shape their Age.

(*The end of the coronation anthem plays. Still blacked out,
the* CHORUS OF THE PAGEANT *sings muted words
from the end of the coronation anthem.*)

Chorus of
the pageant: God of the One shall be
                As the light of the morning.
                God of the One shall speak
                Through the Light.

(*The Light high up above the balcony to the left brightens
and from within it* GOD OF THE ONE *speaks to King
Charles, who is still standing and is in enfolded in bright
Light. The pageant cannot hear the words.*)

God of the One: I care for every creature on my earth,
                 I am with each insect and mammal always,
                 Each of my creations is within my One.
                 I love the painted lady and the deer,
                 I love the barn owl and the ladybird.
                 I love the buzzard and the woodpecker,
                 I love the robin and the daffodil.
                 I love the heron and the winking carp.
                 I care for the poorest poor, and for royals
                 And for the Age they shape, with my One love.
                 I love every event in history.
                 What is history but my One passing through time?
                 The covenant that bestows the divine right

Of kings to shape their Age is still in force.

(*A close-up of the coronation chair in Westminster Abbey is shown on the screen, holding the Stone of Scone under its seat.*)

When Jacob took a stone for a pillow
He dreamed of a ladder reaching to heaven
And angels of God ascending and descending.
The pillow on which he received his dream
Is reputed to be the British Coronation
Stone of Scone, and so it is believed that all
Monarchs crowned on it will receive divine
Guidance, as the covenant guarantees.
You have listened well, Charles, and I am pleased
That in your reign you'll look beyond London
And the territories that are under your rule
To the wider world of all humankind
And will influence the start of the groundwork
That will found a democratic World State
After your reign, that will bring harmony
To those who succeed the Carolingian Age,
On which again I bestow my greetings.
Your soul will soar like an eagle above humankind.

(*The Light floods the throne where King Charles is standing, and then fades and returns to its original brightness.* KING CHARLES *speaks, still standing.*)

King Charles: God of the One and Light, I bow my head
Which will soon be crowned to you, and I promise
My soul will soar like an eagle on the wind,
It will rise higher and higher until I see
The Western hemisphere laid out below,
And it will rise higher to the edge of space.
Like an astronaut I will look down and hold
The turning globe of the earth in my right palm,
A soft ball that's home to all humankind,
And I will look at the earth as you do,
From your perspective and your loving eye.
I solemnly undertake that I will
Dedicate my Carolingian Age

To starting the process, by persuasion,
Of bringing all humankind together
In a new world structure that will embody
World peace and universal harmony.

(*The golden litter is carried in to take King Charles back to his coach so his procession can resume.*)

Epilogue

(Immediately afterwards. On the screen King Charles again sits on the coronation chair in Westminster Abbey. Blackout on the pageant. Minerva is spotlit. The Light high up above the balcony to the left brightens. MINERVA speaks to God of the One within the Light. The pageant cannot hear.)

Minerva: Lord of all, who has always wanted the best
For humankind and has long held a dream,
A vision, of a Golden Age ahead
Of all humankind at peace and in harmony
As in a sunlit meadow of wild flowers,
Which self-interested politicians ignore,
Preferring self-assertive nation-states
To a World State of global citizens,
You wanted to confront flawed humankind
With the disorder in the declining West
And with the fracturing within Europe,
To shock the unruly into improvement,
And in particular confront King Charles
With this problem and show him his solution,
And this I have done to implement your will.
I've shown him how his Carolingian Age
Can be remembered if he takes action,
And his need to urge those who have vision
To begin work on a federal World State
That will come into being and flourish
After his reign has ended, when he's gone.
I've lifted the curtain across the future
And allowed him a peep so he now *knows*.
He has the knowledge, now he needs to act,
To be inspired, consumed with this idea,
To speak to world leaders and the UN,
Scatter influence like poplar fluff in wind.

(The Light above the balcony on the left brightens and floods Minerva. Still blacked out, the CHORUS OF THE PAGEANT sing muted words from the end of the coronation anthem.)

Chorus of
the pageant: God of the One shall be
                As the light of the morning.
                God of the One shall speak
                Through the Light.

                (From within the bright Light GOD OF THE ONE *speaks
                to Minerva. The pageant cannot hear the words.)*

God of the One: Goddess of Wisdom and daughter of Zeus
                 (A protean form of the One that I am),
                 Wise Minerva, your pageant entertainments
                 Excellently showed the chaos within the UK
                 And the suffering among the world's peoples,
                 And you have let King Charles glimpse what he needs
                 To know of his coming Carolingian Age.
                 Owl-eyed, you have shown him a direction.
                 Because we are committed to free will
                 Nothing is fated, Providence is shaped
                 By choices with outcomes, nothing's preordained.
                 King Charles is free to choose whatever course
                 He wishes, but free choice is enmeshed with good
                 Discernment, Knowledge, Vision and Wisdom
                 And you have set him up to be guided
                 By these four virtues while he makes his choice,
                 And if he follows these the right outcome
                 Will lead to a future we can support,
                 Which we have projected and want to see.
                 I gave humankind its freedom, part of me's
                 Always been an Existentialist over
                 Free will. I am now a Universalist
                 Who yearns for universals in structures.
                 I am old and have known deep disappointments:
                 During the last five thousand years each Age,
                 Each grouping within humankind – from tribe
                 To city-state, nation-state and region –
                 Has been misled by ambitious, ruthless men
                 And has fallen victim to cruel conquests
                 And more recently continental wars
                 That have destroyed the churches, temples, mosques
                 That past generations have held sacred,
                 And left them homes for dark-loving bats and mice.

And the destruction of civilisation
Has been carried out by men whose souls have been
Enclosed within the shell of their egos,
As hard as any walnut shell, that resists
The Light I always try to shine into souls.
During the last four hundred years, my Light –
Which was once known in every church or mosque,
In every temple, and taught by holy men,
Monks and desert mystics – has ceased to be known
So humans live in a nourishing mist
Of Light without knowing it's all round them,
Without knowing I love all living forms.
I love all wildlife and all living things
Regardless of the countries they live in,
Regardless of all nation-states' borders,
For they are all creatures within my One.
All living things are citizens of my world.
I love the kingfishers and dragonflies,
I love the primroses and marigolds.
And I love the prickly holly and the rose,
I love the hedgehog and I love the vole.
I love the cherry blossom and the pear.
I love the weeping willow by the stream.
I love the sunflowers and the smiling sun,
I love a field of beaming buttercups,
And I embrace all opposites within
My reconciling, synthesising One
In which all things belong and have a place.
All living forms pass, but species endure.
I worked so hard on the concept of a man,
I designed the human body so carefully.
I got the vocal cords to reflect the lips –
The cords sited downwards, the lips sideways –
And I grasped the solution to proportion:
Beauty's golden ratio, 1.618.
The human mouth is 1.618
Times as wide as the nose; each finger bone
Is 1.618 times its neighbouring bone;
From elbow to wrist is 1.618
Times the distance from wrist to fingertip.
The distance from the navel to the sole
Is 1.618 times the distance

From the top of the head to the navel,
And ideal height's 1.618 times
The distance from shoulder to fingertip.
I crafted the human frame with such precision,
Its ratios were all in perfect proportion.
I took such care in modelling my humans.
I dreamed they'd all be kind, loving and good.
I admire humans, but have reservations.
I admire all humans for what they give,
For their kindness and creativity,
But I do not admire their cruelty,
Their strong belief that they are always right
And are entitled to kill and maim their foes
And conquer peoples and rule through wicked wars
And set themselves above my earth's creatures,
Which they hunt down and kill and devour like beasts.
But some humans retain their love of all
Living beings regardless of borders,
They feel the unity of the universe,
The Oneness of existence on my earth.
They love the earth as I do – nothing can beat
Bees humming in lavender on a summer's day
Or a kestrel hovering still above a field –
But I can't help feeling disillusioned
At the achievements of all humankind
During the last five thousand years, despite
Their high points: Pheidias's perfect statues,
Leonardo's paintings, Beethoven's symphonies,
Shakespeare's plays, the Metaphysical poets.
Again and again humankind's let me down.
And just as we get Europe together,
And a United States of Europe's looming,
The UK shakes the union by heading out.
It's exasperating, I've seen it all before
So many times I groan, "Oh not again."
I don't trust any UK politicians.
That's why I've focused on King Charles, hoping
An enduring royal can see what needs to be done.
I have high hopes of this coronation.
After five thousand years of misplaced hopes –
The Macedonian and Roman Empires,
The Empires of the Franks and the British –

I at last have hopes that the Carolingian Age
Will get beyond the UK and the EU –
A rerun of the Tudor breach with Rome
And the passions of the English Civil War –
And will set humankind on its correct course
By a free-will choice and do the groundwork for
A democratic World State that will bring
A synthesis that will end all conflict,
And a Golden Age, the period of humankind's
Greatest prosperity and high culture,
Literary and artistic merit;
And with fresh Universalist thinking
Abolish war and all nuclear weapons
And bring in a *Pax Universalis*,
A universal peace throughout the world,
That marks for all coming generations
The triumph of universal harmony.

20–23, 27 June; 5, 7–11, 17, 20–24, 26–29 July; 1, 3, 10–14
August; 1–2, 5–10, 17–18, 25, 30–31 October 2019

Notes for *The Coronation of King Charles*

Antimasque

1. For a list of the 72 wars, see Nicholas Hagger, *World State*, pp.268–281.

2. For a list of the 162 wars, see Nicholas Hagger, *World State*, pp.288–293.

Masque

3. For the diagram/flow chart of the structure of the World State, see Nicholas Hagger, *World State*, p.173.

Timeline

List of dates of key events relevant to
The Coronation of King Charles and the Preface

| 14 January 1559 | Elizabeth I's coronation procession through the streets of London on the day before her coronation |

| 25 July 1603 | James I's coronation |

| 15 March 1604 | James I's coronation procession through the streets of London |

| 8 July 1966 | Nicholas Hagger's visit to the Banqueting House |

| 23 June 2016 | UK Referendum, the UK votes to leave the European Union |

| 29 June 2018 | Nicholas Hagger's *World State* and *World Constitution* published |

| 30 October 2018 | Nicholas Hagger's meeting with Grahame Davies, Assistant Private Secretary to The Prince of Wales |

| 22 April 2019 | The first day of the Year of the Phoenix, Nicholas Hagger's speech in Moscow calling for a new era of universal peace |

| 24 July 2019 | Resignation of Theresa May as UK Prime Minister |

| 24 July 2019 | Boris Johnson becomes the UK's Prime Minister and steps up planning for 'no deal' |

| 1 January 2021 | End of transition period, the UK finally leaves the European Union |

APPENDICES

Appendix 1

British Royal Family's Descent from Alfred the Great, 849 to present

38 generations to Charles III via Wessex, Norman, Angevin, Plantagenet, Scottish Stewart, Lancaster, York, Tudor, Stuart, Hanover and Windsor Houses (See pp.4–5)

Dates of kings/queens refer to their reign dates (r.): accession and death. Dates of non-kings/non-queens refer to their birth and death. The direct line of descent is given. Gaps in reign dates indicate that a brother or cousin was on the throne, not a direct ancestor.

Descent from Alfred

1.	Alfred the Great, King of Wessex	r.871–899
2.	Edward the Elder	r.899–924
3.	Edmund I, King of the English	r.939–946
4.	Edgar I, the Peaceful King of England	r.959–975
5.	Æthelred the Unready, King of the English	r.978–1013 and r.1014–1016
6.	Edmund II, King of the English	r.1016
7.	Edward the Exile	1016–1057
8.	Margaret of Scotland	c.1045–1093
9.	Matilda of Scotland, m. Henry I of House of Normandy, King of England	c.1080–1118
10.	Matilda	r.1141 (reigned 208 days)
11.	Henry II of House of Plantagenet	r.1154–1189

12.	King John	r.1199–1216
13.	Henry III	r.1216–1272
14.	Edward I, Longshanks	r.1272–1307
15.	Edward II	r.1307–1327
16.	Edward III	r.1327–1377
17.	John of Gaunt of House of Lancaster, 1st Duke of Lancaster	1340–1399
18.	John Beaufort, 1st Earl of Somerset, younger brother of Henry IV	1373–1410
19.	John Beaufort, 1st Duke of Somerset, cousin of Henry V	1403–1444
20.	Margaret Beaufort, Countess of Richmond and Derby, cousin of Henry VI, m. Rhys ap Gruffydd	1441/1443–1509
21.	Henry VII of House of Tudor, born in Wales	r.1485–1509
22.	Margaret Tudor, elder sister of Henry VIII	1489–1541
23.	James V of Scotland	1512–1542
24.	Mary Queen of Scots	1542–1587
25.	James VI of Scotland and I of England	r.1567–1625 (Scotland) r.1603–1625 (England)
26.	Elizabeth Electress Palatine, elder sister of Charles I	1596–1662
27.	Sophia of Hanover, Electress of Brunswick	1630–1714
28.	George I of House of Hanover	r.1714–1727

29. George II   r.1727–1760

30. Frederick Prince of Wales   1707–1751

31. George III   r.1760–1820

32. Edward Duke of Kent and Strathearn,
    younger brother of George IV and
    William IV   1767–1820

33. Queen Victoria   r.1837–1901

34. Edward VII of House of Windsor (House
    of Saxe-Coburg and Gotha)   r.1901–1910

35. George V   r.1910–1936

36. George VI, younger brother of Edward VIII   r.1936–1952

37. Elizabeth II   r.1952–

38. Charles III   1948–

Appendix 2

Royal Descent from King David the Psalmist, c.1010BC to present

123 generations to Charles III (See pp.9–10)

Dates of kings/queens refer to their reign dates: accession and death. Spellings of Biblical names are taken from the King James Version of the Bible, with Hebrew spellings sometimes in brackets. The list below is of generations and omits accessions of siblings, for example a brother and uncle between 609BC and 586BC, and the brothers Edward VIII and George VI in 1936.

Legendary/historical Biblical descent before David

1. Adam   Eve

2. Seth

3. Enos

4. Cainan

5. Mahalaleel

6. Jared

7. Enoch

8. Methuselah

9. Lamech

10. Noah   Naamah

11. Shem

12. Arphaxad

13. Salah

14. Heber

15. Peleg

16. Reu

17. Serug

18. Nahor

19. Terah   Amtheta

20. Abraham   Sarah

21. Isaac   Rebekah

22. Jacob   Leah

23. Judah   Tamar

24. Pharez (or Perez)

25. Hezron

26. Aram (or Ram)

27. Amminadab

28. Naashon (or Nahshon)

29. Salmon

30. Boaz   Ruth

31. Obed

32. Jesse

Kings of Judah

33.	King David, King of Judah and Israel, King Saul's favourite	c.1010–970BC	Bathsheba
34.	King Solomon, King of Judah and Israel	c.970–931BC	Naamah
35.	King Rehoboam, King of Judah	c.931–913BC	Maacah
36.	King Abijam	c.913–911BC	
37.	King Asa	c.911–870BC	Azubah
38.	King Jehoshaphat	c.870–849BC	
39.	King Jehoram	c.849–842BC	Athaliah
40.	King Ahaziah	c.842–841BC	Zibiah
41.	King Joash	c.836–796BC	Jehoaddan
42.	King Amaziah	c.796–767BC	Jecholiah
43.	King Uzziah	c.767–742BC	Jerushah
44.	King Jotham	c.742–735BC	
45.	King Ahaz	c.735–716BC	Abi
46.	King Hezekiah	c.716–687BC	Hephzibah
47.	King Manasseh	c.687–643BC	Meshullemeth
48.	King Amon	c.643–640BC	Jedidah
49.	King Josiah	c.640–609BC	

50.	King Zedekiah, last King of Judah	c.597–586BC	

Kings of Ireland

51.	King Heremon	fl.580BC	Tea Tephi,[1] daughter of Zedekiah, m. c.586BC, became Queen of Ireland on 21 June 583BC
52.	King Irial Faidh (or Iriel Faid)	r.10 years	
53.	King Eithriall (or Ethriel)	r.20 years	
54.	Follain (or Follach)		
55.	King Tighernmas (or Tigernmas)	r.50 years	
56.	Eanbotha		
57.	Smiorguil		
58.	King Fiachadh Labhriane	r.24 years	
59.	King Aongus Ollmuchaidh	r.21 years	
60	Maoin		
61.	King Rotheachta	r.25 years	
62.	Dein		
63.	King Siorna Saoghalach	r.21 years	
64.	Oholla Olchaoin		

65. King Giallebadh r.9 years

66. King Aodhain Glas r.20 years

67. King Simeon Breac r.6 years

68. King Muireadach Bolgrach r.4 years

69. King Fiachadh Tolgrach r.7 years

70. King Duach Laidhrach r.10 years

71. Eochaidh Buaigllcrg

72. King Ugaine[2] More the r.30 years
    Great

73. King Cobhthach Coalbreag r.30 years

74. Meilage

75. King Jaran Gleofathaeb r.7 years

76. King Coula Cruaidh r.4 years
    Cealgach

77. King Oiliolla r.25 years
    Caisfhiachach

78. King Eochaidh r.11 years
    Foltleathan

79. King Aongus Tuirmheach r.30 years
    Teamharch[3]

80. King Eana Aighneach r.28 years

81. Labhra Luire

82. Blathuchta

83. Easamhuin Eamhua

84. Roighnein Ruadh

85. Finlogha

86. Fian

87. King Eodchaidh Feidhlioch   r.12 years

88. Fineamhuas

89. King Lughaidh Riadhdearg

90. King Criombthan Niadhnar   r.16 years

91. Fearaidhach Fion
    Feachtnuigh

92. King Fiaebadh Fionoluidh   r.20 years

93. King Tuathal Teachtmar   r.50 years

94. King Coun Ceadchatbach   r.20 years

95. King Arb Aonflier   r.30 years

96. King Cormae Usada   r.40 years

97. King Caibre Liffeachair   r.27 years

98. King Fiachadh Sreabthuine   r.30 years

99. King Muireadhach Tireach   r.30 years

100. King Eochaidh   r.7 years
    Moigmeodhin

101. King Niall of the Nine
    Hostages

102. King Eogan macNeill   d.465AD

103.	King Muireadhach of Dal Riata (or Dairiada)	r. c.465–489AD
104.	King Earea of Dal Riata (Eric of Dairiada)	r. c.489–498AD

Kings of Argyllshire

105.	King Feargus More (Fergus Mor, son of Eric of Dairiada)[4]	487AD	
106.	King Dongard	d.457	
107.	King Conran	d.535	
108.	King Aidan	d.604	
109.	King Eugene IV	d.622	
110.	King Donald IV	d.650	
111.	Dongard		
112.	King Eugene V	d.692	
113.	Findan		
114.	King Eugene VII	d.721	Spondan
115.	King Effinus	d.761	Fergina
116.	King Achaius	d.819	Fergusia
117.	King Alpin	d.834	

Sovereigns of Scotland

118.	King Kenneth I (or Kinadius, son of King Alpin)	r.834–858, King of Dal Riata (Dairiada, 834–858), conqueror of the Picts, King of the Picts 843–858	
119.	King Constantin II	d.874	
120.	King Donald VI	d.903	
121.	King Malcolm I	d.958	
122.	King Kenneth II[5]	d.995	
123.	King Malcolm II	d.1033	
124.	Beatrix		m.Thane Albanach
125.	King Duncan I	d.1040	
126.	King Malcolm III Canmore	1055–1093	Margaret of England
127.	King David I	d.1153	Maud of Northumberland
128.	Prince Henry	d.1152	Adama of Surrey
129.	Earl David	d.1219	Maud of Chester
130.	Isobel		m.Robert Bruce III
131.	Robert Bruce IV		m.Isobel of Gloucester
132.	Robert Bruce V		m.Martha of Carriok
133.	King Robert I Bruce	r.1306–1329	Mary of Burke

134. Marjorie Bruce		m.Walter Stewart III	
135. King Robert II	d.1390	Euphemia of Ross	d.1376
136. King Robert III	d.1406	Arabella Drummond	d.1401
137. King James I	1424–1437	Joan Beaufort	
138. King James II	d.1460	Margaret of Gueldres	d.1463
139. King James III	d.1488	Margaret of Denmark	d.1484
140. King James IV	d.1543	Margaret of England	d.1539
141. King James V	d.1542	Mary of Lorraine	d.1560
142. Queen Mary (Mary, Queen of Scots)	d.1587	Henry, Lord Darnley	

Sovereigns of Great Britain
and after 1801 the United Kingdom

143. King James VI Stuart and I	r.1603–1625	Anne of Denmark	
144. Princess Elizabeth Stuart	1596–1613	Frederick V, King of Bohemia, Elector Palatine[6]	
145. Princess Sophia of the Palatinate and of Hanover, Electress of Brunswick	d.1714	m.Ernest Augustus, Duke of Brunswick-Lüneburg	
146. King George I of the House of Hanover	1698–1727	Sophia Dorothea of Zelle	1667–1726

147.	King George II	1727–1760	Princess Caroline of Ansbach	1683–1737
148.	Prince Frederick, Prince of Wales[7]	1707–1751	Princess Augusta of Saxe-Gotha	
149.	King George III	r.1760–1820	Princess Sophia of Mecklenburg-Strelitz	1744–1818
150.	Edward, Duke of Kent	1767–1820	Victoria, daughter of the Duke of Saxe-Coburg-Saalfeld, widow of the Prince of Leiningen	
151.	Queen Victoria	b.1819, r. 1837–1901	Prince Albert of Saxe-Coburg, began House of Saxe-Coburg-Gotha, renamed House of Windsor	
152.	King Edward VII	r.1901–1910	Princess Alexandra	
153.	King George V	r.1910–1936	Princess Mary of Teck	
154.	King George VI	r.1936–1952	Lady Elizabeth Bowes-Lyon	
155.	Queen Elizabeth II	r.1952–	Prince Philip of Greece and Denmark, Duke of Edinburgh	
156.	King Charles III	b.1948	1. Lady Diana Spencer; Diana, Princess of Wales 2. Camilla Shand (m. Andrew Parker Bowles), Duchess of Cornwall	

Notes on Descent

1. Tea Tephi was a daughter of King Zedekiah, who was taken captive to Babylon and had his eyes put out. His two daughters Tea Tephi and Tamar Tephi were placed under the guardianship of Jeremiah the prophet. After the destruction of Jerusalem in 587/586BC they were taken to Egypt and put in charge of smuggled-out sacred Hebrew treasures, and Jeremiah's scribe found a ship so they could leave Egypt with the Ark of the Covenant, King David's harp and Jacob's pillow stone. This was the stone pillow on which the head of Jacob rested at Bethel. According to tradition it had become the capstone of the Temple in Jerusalem and had been taken to Egypt by Jacob's sons and later became the coronation stone: the red-sandstone Stone of Destiny, the Stone of Scone. They reached Ireland and Tea Tephi married Heremon Eochaid, King of Ireland, who was descended from the House of Judah (Jacob's fourth son Judah, his son Zarah and grandson Caled). She and her sister were known as the Princesses of the Harp. The Irish Kings were crowned sitting on the Stone of Destiny. The Scotti (Gaelic) tribe in Ireland took the coronation Stone of Destiny to Argyllshire in south-west Scotland, where it became the coronation stone of the Scottish kings. Edward I took it from Scotland in 1296, and it then became the coronation stone of the British monarchs. It was therefore the coronation stone for the kings of Ireland, Scotland and England. It was returned to Scotland in 1996, 700 years after it was removed to England.

2. The Scottish royal male line descends from Ugaine Mor the Great, the 66th High King of Ireland according to medieval Irish legend and historical tradition.

3. There is also a second line of Irish descent via Fiachra-firmara to Eric Dairiada.

4. There is also a second line of Scottish descent via King Gabran to King Alpin.

5. There is also a third line of Scottish descent via Kenneth II's daughter Dunclina – Banquo, Thane of Lochaber, d.1043AD – Fleance, b.1020AD – Walter, Thane of Lochaber – Alan of Lochaber – Walter Fitzalan, 1st High Steward of Scotland, d.1177AD – Alan Fitzwalter, 2nd High Steward of Scotland – Walter Stewart, 3rd High Steward of Scotland – Alexander Stewart, 4th High Steward of Scotland – Sir James Stewart,

5th High Steward of Scotland – Sir Walter Stewart, 6th High Steward of Scotland, m. Marjorie Bruce, daughter of Robert I Bruce of Scots (see 133). (Shakespeare explored all three lines of the Scottish descent of James I in *Macbeth*, which includes Banquo, Fleance and King Duncan I, who was killed by Macbeth.)

6. The wedding of Elizabeth Stuart, James I's daughter, and Frederick V took place in the royal chapel at the Palace of Whitehall on 14 February 1613. Shakespeare's patron, the 3rd Earl of Southampton, accompanied her to Heidelberg Castle, where a replica of the Globe theatre was built. The British royal family is descended from this Palatinate marriage.

7. There is also a second line of Welsh descent through the Welsh royal houses traditionally from Anna, daughter of St James (half-brother of Jesus from Joseph's previous marriage, see apocryphal *Gospel of James*), and more certainly from Charlemagne and the Hereditary Stewards of Dol (both male descendants of the House of Judah).

Works referred to include: Geoffrey Keating, *History of Ireland*, Dublin, 1723; James Anderson, *Royal Genealogies*, London, 1732; Sharon Turner, *History of the Anglo-Saxons*, Vol.1, 1799; C.V. Lavoisne, *Genealogical and Historical Atlas*, London, 1814; Rev. F.R.A. Glover, *England, the Remnant of Judah and the Israel of Ephraim*, London, 1861; J.C. Stephens, *Genealogical Chart, shewing the Connection between the House of David and the Royal Family of Britain*, Liverpool, 1877; H. Polano, *The Talmud*, London, 1877; Rev. A.B. Grimaldi, *Forty-Seven Identifications of the British with Lost Israel*, 1885; and J.H. Allen, *Judah's Sceptre and Joseph's Birthright*, 1902.

Appendix 3

54 Commonwealth Countries
(See pp.16–18)

Taken from http://thecommonwealth.org/member-countries

Countries by region:

Africa
- Botswana
- Cameroon
- Gambia, The
- Ghana
- Kenya
- Kingdom of Eswatini
- Lesotho
- Malawi
- Mauritius
- Mozambique
- Namibia
- Nigeria
- Rwanda
- Seychelles
- Sierra Leone
- South Africa
- Uganda
- United Republic of Tanzania
- Zambia

Asia
- Bangladesh
- Brunei Darussalam
- India
- Malaysia
- Maldives
- Pakistan
- Singapore
- Sri Lanka

Caribbean and Americas
- Antigua and Barbuda

- Bahamas, The
- Barbados
- Belize
- Canada
- Dominica
- Grenada
- Guyana
- Jamaica
- Saint Lucia
- St Kitts and Nevis
- St Vincent and The Grenadines
- Trinidad and Tobago

Europe
- Cyprus
- Malta
- United Kingdom

Pacific
Australia
- Fiji
- Kiribati
- Nauru
- New Zealand
- Papua New Guinea
- Samoa
- Solomon Islands
- Tonga
- Tuvalu
- Vanuatu

BOOKS

O-BOOKS

O is a symbol of the world, of oneness and unity; this eye represents knowledge and insight.